song of ourself

Song of Ourself

VOICES IN UNISON

DRAGOLIN
INDIE PRESS

Dragolin Indie Press
P.O. Box 750
Prosser, WA 99350

Ordering Information: Special discounts are available on quantity purchases by corporations, associations, and others. For details, contact the publisher at the address above.

Bend, OR — First Edition

ISBN 978-0-578-46673-6

Printed in the United States of America

Cover art: Photograph by Emma Hunter.

Some names and identifying details have been changed to protect the privacy of individuals.
To honor the international scope of writers brought together here, national conventions for spelling and punctuation have been retained throughout.

Kindred Spirit, 2017
By Tracey Hewitt
Mixed media and collage on watercolor paper
www.traceyhewitt.com

I celebrate myself, and sing myself,
And what I assume you shall assume,
For every atom belonging to me as good belongs to you.

- Walt Whitman, "Song of Myself"

TABLE OF CONTENTS

PART I: AWAKENING

Invitation

The Invitation by Rebecca Tolin	7
What If by Ashley Ellington Brown	8
What Will You Brave? by Marianne Collins	11
Universe's Menu by Carmela Fleury	14
Spring Cleaning by Heather Barninger	16
Permission Not Required by Jennifer Izumi	18
A Letter to the Newly Diagnosed by Debee DiMenichi	19
A Gift for You and the Healing of the World by Fernanda Lodeiro	24
All Things Shall Be Revealed... by Dawn Van Dyck	26
Verve by Melissa Pratt	28
In the Game Operators' Lunch Room by Sylke Laine	29
From Behind the Veil by Diane Roberson Douiyssi	31

Recognition

Excited to See You by Rebecca Liu	33
I Am Joan of Arc by Laurel Morales	35
Confessions of a Fake News Manufacturer by Anisha Imhasly	37
Entropy and Evolution in One by Tia H. Ho	39
Beauty Within the Beast by Sandi Means	42
The Reluctant Genie by Katja Svensson	44
Confessions of a Flight Risk by Danielle E. Fournier	45
Satanic Airlines Flight 666 to Hell by Emma Campbell Webster	47
Prayer by Anna Smith	49
Garden of the Parallels by Corry Angwar	51
Esker by Tricia Elliott	52
Flying With My Father by Usha Rani Sharma	54

Acceptance

How I Frack Myself by Mia Brown	56
Ignoring the Stubble by Leah Carey	58
Ode to Old Lady Arm by E. B. Brown	60
Wild by Annelie Ferreira	62
How I Got Rid of my "Sure-I-Can-Do-That-For-You" Scarf and "You-Can-Rely-On-Me-For-Everything" Hat by Kaliopi Nikitas	64

The Dirty Bathroom by Blossom Lievore   66
The Truth Was Wary of Her by Laura Harbin   68
The Golden Ticket by Kim Smith   70
Enough by Kat Soong   72
Croning by Jill Syme   74
Finding Freedom by Tracey Hewitt   76

Reclamation

The Truth of You Does Not Need to Be Contained:
An Ode to Those with Rubbermaid Bins Stacked Neatly
in the Closet by Kate Godin   78
Conversation With a Whale by Aubri Tallent   79
This Morning the Dam Broke by Alison Oresman Wilson   81
Garnet by Lauren Oujiri   82
La Planchadora by Kimberly Blanchard   85
The Substance of My Soul by Guiomar Holme   86
We Decided to Exist by Meagan Adele Lopez   88
The Truth by Joy Brill   91
the gift of no by Cristine Reynaert   92
Into the World by Rachel Bruns   93
How Silvermoon Found Her Heart, Her Purpose and a
Friend by Leigh Ann Kittell   95
I Finally Tell My Truth by Cindy Lou Levee/ Natanya   97
Lucky Fish by Melissa Pennel   99
The Path to Our True Selves: A Letter
for the Journey by Hyeon-Ju Rho   101

PART II: BECOMING

Overcoming

Mammal That You Are by Julie Finelli   107
Very Superstitious by Tonya Collings Crombie   108
Reconciliation by Rhonda Jean Seiter   110
Traveling Notes for This Abyss by Shana Brodnax   113
To You, the Person Heading Into the Abyss by Ingrid Bizio   115
Postcard From the Ledge by Allyson Linehan   116
LIFEJacket by Tracy Weber, Ph.D.   118
The Light Through the Window by Keri Clarke   120
The Agony, The Shift, The Blessing by Lois Melkonian   121

The Journey by LK Toepfer   123
Forward by Francine Yacintha   126
Canyon Gift Shop Now Open by Kate DeSmet   128

Surrender

King Arthur's Cave by Emma Hunter   131
Remember by Pat Johnson   133
How to Survive a Rip Current (And Other Life
Crises) by Annie Ferguson Muscato   134
Surviving the Abyss of Infancy by Emily Rosen Rittenberg   136
To Free My Captive Soul by Deanna De Paoli   138
When There's a Monster in the Abyss by Linda Jackson   139
Aphorisms on Writing and Life by Kris Bell   140
(Im) Patience by Anna Bruk   142
Chaos by Crystal Pirri   143
You are the Horse by Jennifer Shryock   145

Transformation

The Becoming by DK Crawford   147
Wingspan by Noelle Newby   150
Cake by Jenn Stuart   152
Three Wishes by Paula Boone   154
Once Upon a Game of Chess by Dr. Irina Kotlar   156
Life as a Zero Sum Game by Amanda Chudak   158
I Am Curious by Marion Perepolkin   159
Three Stillnesses by Shelby Bach   160
Cold Floors and Blueberry Bread by Becky Flynn   163
Between Worlds by Liz Wiltzen   165
Mystery by Amanda Cooke   168

Renewal

Sestina: When we were young and green by Elizabeth Spelman   171
For Everything There Is A Season by Julianne May   173
Lying Fallow by Carol Finch   176
And Yet by Leslie K Sullivan   177
Changing Frequencies by Angela Housley   178
Discovering Recovery by Laurie Swanson   179
The Permission Slip by Kim Brahm Oswald   180
Born Anew by Naina Saligram   182
In Between by Susan A. Ring   184
Born into Death, and Gentle Illumination by Jeana Bird   185

PART III: CONNECTING

Remembrance

Approaching Dust by Michelle Wells 191
Eulogy of a Wild Girl by Clare Allen 193
Uncle Karyk's Cottage by Jindra Cekan 195
A Note From My Mom, And Maybe Yours by Carrie Seid 197
Midden by Jessica Waite 198
ENOUGH by Ceridwyn Mizera 200
Gift Her With Eyes That Look Soft On Her Pain by Carol Bonneville 201
Rhinanthus minor by Arwen Niles 203
Etheric Bands of Connectivity Through Time
by Judith Elaine Halek–Thriver 206
Eternal Return by Bettina M. Stuetz 208
Love Will Sustain You by Clare Smart 210

Communion

I AM HERE by Susan Telford 213
Vessels of Light by Pamela Rae 216
if I could write a word by mab 217
A Letter to My White People by Hannah du Plessis 218
July Morning by Cynthia Rome 220
North Star Speaks by Anastasia Brencick, MA, LMP 222
Spirit Horse by Jane Waugh 223
Vesper by Colleen Raine 224
Rooted by Love by Jenny Lee Rowe 227
Wild Creature by Fatima Viola 229
Homecoming by Tracy Cottrell 230

Immanence

Once in a Lifetime, Same as it Ever Was by Judith Stewart 233
Already There by Johanne Lila Larsen 235
Finding Our Voices by Katrina Allen 237
The Secret of Stars by Wendy Wyatt 239
Perfection by Linda Amato 241
Nature's Symphony by E.L. (Betsy) Kudlinski 242
Feather by Mary Walker 244
Crayon by Barbara Barnett 245
A Book's Tale by Seja Ateia 246
Dog Hair Stories by Anne Woods 248
Praise Song for the Gubudubu by Melanie Phoenix 250

Transcendence

Come Out and Play, Spirit by Mer Boel   254
The Everythingy by Alise James   256
A Letter From God by Akumi Yokoyama   258
Please Stay Very Close by Mary Geer   259
A Hospice Nurse / Novelist / Activist's Prayer by Emunah Herzog   260
Lead Them Home by Kelly Berg   263
Human in Nature by Kerryn Elrick   265
Way of Life—The Artist's Way (A Villanelle) by Elina van der Heijden   266
In and After by Mary Cartledgehayes   268
Out of Exile by Elsa Wolman Katana   269
When I Am Free by Kathy McKinley   270
I call canon in the rock cathedral by Lara O'Connor   272

PREFACE

In 2017, hundreds of people from around the world embarked on a transformative experiment called "Write into Light," led by visionary author Martha Beck. While we learned much about writing, the course ultimately sought to create a new paradigm for living. Most powerfully, the message *you are never alone* rang like the daily bell of truth. In the safe sanctum of an emergent community, separated by space but united by love, we came to confide our failures, confusion, grief, trauma, triumphs, wonders, and joy, finding mirrors of our stories in the lives and voices of those we had never actually met but whom we intimately knew as *us*.

You are never alone.

It is with this as our guiding principle that we wanted to share our words with each other, and with you.

The title of this anthology derives from Walt Whitman's famous "Song of Myself," an existential celebration of identity and communion. At the end of the first stanza, Whitman declares oneness as his fundamental principle: "for every atom belonging to me as good belongs to you." The speaker throughout finds himself embedded in the experience of all—the animate and the inanimate, the living and the dead, the past and the present. Boundaries are erased; *I* dissolves into *We*; *Self* is recast as *Ourself*.

Ourself is not yet a word recognized in the English language. Nonetheless, we felt it necessary to capture the ideal we are striving for—not multiple selves, but rather one shared self, expressed and vitalized through the many. The notion is in some ways counter to conventional ways of thinking, but when challenging cultural norms, a new vocabulary is often needed.

The arc of transformation from *myself* to *ourself* is the overarching theme of this anthology. We trace the alchemy of internal creation: the Awakening and Becoming of one's truest self and, ultimately, the path of Connecting to the world at large. As Maya Angelou said, "we delight in the beauty of the butterfly, but rarely admit the changes it has gone through to achieve that beauty." When caterpillars undergo radical change, they dis-integrate and then rebuild. In emerging anew, they re-integrate the relationships not only inside themselves, but also with their environment. They take their place in what Mary Oliver has coined the "family of things." The pieces assembled here were born in a similar spirit of kinship.

Collectively, we struggle, we try to gain momentum, we fail, we fall…then out of nowhere help arrives as an internal or external embrace. It's a beautiful circle, that we might write and you might be there to catch our fragile words in the net of your consciousness. It is in this circle that the fabric of our intertwining is unveiled. We, the universe, sing in unison.

In the following pages, we tread a path of self-discovery; we find light in our darkest hours, dipping in and out of moments of fear, vulnerability, and courage. We take solace in the compassion of friends, open our eyes to the extraordinary in the ordinary, and seek peace in the beauty of a higher plane. This is a portrait of the lived human experience, in all its devastation and glory.

This is the Song of Ourself.

I.
*A*WAKENING

Sempervivum Hybrid Black
Photograph by Heather Barninger
hbarninger.smugmug.com

INVITATION

The Invitation
By Rebecca Tolin

Providence knocks.

You open the door to see
a needy beast on your doorstep
with your name and a handwritten note scrawled
Begin.

You didn't order loss or ruin,
the shattering of a tidy life.
But here it is,
with its own heft and reason.

The invitation is this —
Whatever the burden, wherever it came from,
carry it in your capable arms,
wrap it with your wild curiosity.

Live as if you chose it.

Rebecca Tolin enjoys tree gazing, trail blazing, word playing, twisting into new shapes, communing with loved ones, asking the unanswerable questions, and drifting in the silence that gives rise to it all.

What If
By Ashley Ellington Brown

What if you believed you are worthy?
What if you accepted the praise rather than deflecting it?
What if you embraced the joy as much as you assume the pain?

What if you agreed that you are special,
that inside you lives a gorgeous spirit nothing can break,
that you are more than enough just as you are?

What if the only person you need to hear that from is you?

What if you trusted in the love that yearns toward you,
in the light that others seem to see?
What if you believed that people you admire could admire you?

What if you believed that you make a difference?

What if you stopped holding yourself back,
pushing yourself down,
making yourself small?

What if you allowed the glory biding its time offstage to step into the
spotlight?

What if you felt the terror and did it anyway,
faced the hurt and kept on going,
broke down the door and pushed your way free?

What if believing in yourself was as natural as believing in the sunrise?

What if you understood that mountains in your path are not meant to block
your way,
but rather to elevate you to a higher vantage point
from which you can see more clearly?

What if you took that leap of faith despite your crippling fear of heights?

What if you gave up needing to know,
insisting on being right,
being afraid to fail?

What if you stopped hiding your tears — and your smiles?

What if you opened yourself up,
laid yourself bare,
and stayed that way without resisting?

What if you gave yourself the triumph of surviving your worst nightmare?

What if you shared it all,
gave everything away,
and expected nothing in return?

What do you think might come to you?

What if you relaxed,
and rested,
and laid down your heavy burden of *should*?

What new delights might be waiting for you?

What if you LET GO —
every second of every minute
of every day?

What magic might land on your fingertips?

What if you stopped trying so hard —
or stopped trying at all —
and started allowing?

What sort of miracle might brush against your cheek?

What if you opened the faucet all the way,
unkinked the hose,
and set the nozzle on full?

What magnificence might pour forth?

What if you stopped insisting that you're all alone,
that you have no power,
that you're ordinary?

What if the teacher you seek is actually inside you?

What if you gave up?
What if you gave in?
What if you stopped swimming and started floating, trusting in your natural buoyancy and the path of the current?

On what golden shore might you land?

Ashley Ellington Brown is a writer, dreamer, and constant seeker. She is the author of the blog Joy Detectives and the book A Beautiful Morning: How a Morning Ritual Can Feed Your Soul and Transform Your Life. Ashley lives in Florida with her husband and son.
www.abeautifulmorningbook.com/
www.joydetectives.com/

What Will You Brave?
By Marianne Collins

Step right up! Come all! Come one!
It's time to play. Let's have some fun.

Yes you, Sir, with the furrowed brow,
all bent on force and your know-how,
so powerless, with strengths unused,
chock full of facts and still confused.

And you, Ma'am, with the attaché,
your troubled eyes so far away,
big blinders on, under the gun,
you need this, too, like anyone.

And you, there, with your squandered past,
full of regret that gifts don't last,
so much of life slipped through your hands,
you had your sights on other plans.

What's offered here will blow your mind,
especially if it's been unkind.
Here systems fall and worlds unfold,
and every concept ever told
will break to pieces by your hand,
and fractal worlds form at command,
swift change makers lean into turns,
and precious truths will be unlearned.

What's this you say? How can that be?
Hello there, Curiosity!

If truth be told, I've not a clue
of what's inside, that's up to you:
a tiny bird upon your knee,
a thousand moons in cups of tea,
a common love, a true New Earth,
where energy can now give birth
to joy and grace and love so true
that all can see that i am you.

The question is: What will you brave?
Will you live wild? Or just behave?
Domestication's been your lot.
Just look at all the woe *that's* brought.
To have that gone, what would you pay?
The price is right to have you play.

The cost to you? No more than change,
not from your pocket, from your brain.
Just leave your mindset at the door.
Lay all untruths there on the floor.
Your social norms, discard them, too,
and all that stuff that isn't you.

But fear not, Child, you'll have a guide,
a fierce Enchantress by your side.
She'll caution you to free your brain
from all its thinking, so constrained,
But for courageous hearts intent
on driving change — beWILDerment
will be your best tool and your bliss...
I've said enough! It's down to this:

I've known your fear, I've felt your pain.
You've naught to lose and all to gain.
The part of you that's light and true
is speaking now, knows what to do.
There is no doubt, no words to say.
Just step right up! C'mon! Let's play!

Marianne loves unbridled laughter, ridiculous rhymes, and the wild ride of a learning curve. A lover of change, she is surprised to find herself often living on Vancouver Island.

Following Joy
By Anneli Davey
Acrylic on canvas

Universe's Menu
By Carmela Fleury

What would you like to order today?

******STARTERS******

Security

It's never too late to have a happy childhood. You still have a choice.
Set and draw boundaries. You are safe and divinely protected.

Belonging

Whatever warms your heart and soul is where you belong. You are perfectly lovable
exactly as you are. Give and receive affection. Treasure your precious, worthy self.

Original Gifts

You are unique. Nurture yourself. You have everything you need to manifest your
intentions. You have an amazingly capable brain and body.
You are highly creative by nature.
Know the original gifts that you bring into this world and use them to serve others.

******MAINS******

Love

Have a lifelong love affair with yourself. Love wins, love always wins.
You are deeply loved.
Always.

Trust

Hurt people hurt. Free people free.
Follow the free ones.
The ones with the genuine laughter, who make you feel oxygenated, positive and light.
Believe in the power of magic and synchronicity. Don't worry about down the road.
You are perfect where you are. Now.
You are being divinely guided. Accept life without judgment or criticism.

******SIDES******

Intuition

Empower your own inner wisdom. You can always awaken your intuition.
Self-healing energy is limitless.

Help

There is no wrong time to ask for help and support. Or to provide help and support.
Lighting someone else's candle with your flame doesn't turn yours off.
Help brings blessings to all those around you.

******DESSERTS******

The Sweetness of Life

Take pleasure in the small things in life. Appreciate the energy of a wonderful healer.
The taste of a delicious meal. The wonder of the beauty all around you.
Right now. Buddha Smile. Meditate. Breathe deeply.
Enjoy all the things that don't live in a consumer culture.

******DRINKS******

Joy

You deserve a life of joy and fulfillment.
Have your eyes meet with the oneness of the universe.
Flirt. Have a glass of wine together. Make it a bottle. Dance.
Admit to having high school crushes on each other. Laugh together. Come into unity.
Now. Here. Go on a spiritual journey and procreate.

******KIDS' MENU******

Nature

Nature is divine presence constantly reminding you to be in the moment. Always renew
your appreciation and respect for Mother Nature, especially around children.

All subjective to a 10% tax with sickness, 20% with aging, and 100% with death.
Enjoy!

Carmela Fleury is a certified Martha Beck Life Coach and a certified Holistic Health
Coach from the Institute of Integrative Nutrition. She is training with Sarah Powers to
become a certified Insight Yoga Teacher. She has a soft spot for working with
mothers of young children and currently leads "Raising Happy & Healthy Mamas"
retreats worldwide. <u>www.carmelafleury.com</u>

Spring Cleaning
By Heather Barninger

Inhale,

AaaaCHoo… Sneeze out the dust!

'Suck it up buttercup,' *with the Hoover that is.*

Get the rag bag and wipe away those coffee rings,

And leave a citrusy fresh scent in the air, Ha!

Match Frida's unfaltering gaze as the monkey relaxes on her shoulder,

Surrounded by her denizens of the jungle you just entered into.

Stack the magazines to keep, and get started on the teetering piles of paperwork…

To Do, To File, Too Old to Bother…

Use a discerning eye and keep the heavy duty trash bag close by.

Make space on the desk for…space.

Finish something, and I don't mean that six-month-old caramel you just found under the Post-it notes.

Finish your thought.

Finish what you can, and move on.

Clear away the cobwebs in the darkened corners of the ceiling,

And vacuum up the upended fly carcass on the sill.

There's no more time for procrastinating.

Fix the broken blind and let the light stream in,

Who cares if a whoosh of dust motes flies?

The dog wants a sunny spot to curl up in.

Throw up the window and listen to the fluttering wings

Of your feathered friends vying for the most prominent seat at their copper restaurant.

Feel the breeze on your face and hear the Oaks creak,

Stretch your able, if aging, hands to the ceiling, raising your magic wand,

'*Abracadabra, alakazam...*' with a flourish,

Release the Circus Elephant who has taken residence on your chest.

Inhale.

Feel your scalp tingle.

Unclench.

Shrug your shoulders, Atlas has it covered.

Exhale.

Let the sobs of a thousand years out.

Let your vertebrae align and your hips sigh.

Sit.

Stay.

Find *your* way.

Heather Barninger is Mom to a sage (Zoe) and a sprite (Max), both still in elementary and who already know everything; Director of Marketing by trade and Award-Winning (local contests) Nature Photographer during any free time. Unsure where she's going, but still hoping to stumble upon the meaning of everything.

Permission Not Required
By Jennifer Izumi

Sister, we can't hear you
Your lips are sealed with glue.

Sister, embrace your own caress
And let your throat undress.

Sister, do not be so shy
Let your eyes look up high.

Sister, do not be afraid
Dare yourself out of the shade.

Sister, don't wait for permission
Turn on your heart's ignition.

Sister, turn up that volume
And let your song bloom.

Sister, revel in the freedom to roam
For you are back now — back at home.

Bookworm and baker and beer connoisseur; loves to read a breathtaking book with buttered biscuits and Belgiany beer.

A Letter to the Newly Diagnosed
By Debee DiMenichi

Write, darling.
Write.
Every.
Fucking.
Detail
of your agony.
Carve
your losses
into the page.
Soak them
with the tears
of your
disappointment.

You
are worth
all
the time
it takes
to get
well.

Step back.

Witness
it all
from a distance.

Put away the
number two
pencil.
This is not
a test,
but
an invitation
to love
yourself
more,
an invitation
to give

sweetness
access
to your pain.

An invitation
to learn
the subtle,
but
life-changing
difference
between
checking up
and
checking in.

Study
the great forgivers.
Ask
for the recipe
of their balm.

You will need it
when you break
your own
heart.
And you will break it.

But less and less
as you receive and
give mercy
to you.

Do your best
not to use
your illness
as an excuse
or currency.
Excuses are
kryptonite.

Dare to step into your power.

Healers of all
sizes and shapes
will arrive
at your door.
Some will be
the real deal.
Some,
snake oil
salesmen.
Invite them in.
They are
reflections
of you.

Fortune tellers will
predict
blindness.
Stroke.
Amputation.

Unbutton your blouse
and gaze
into the heart
of your own
crystal ball.
Linger there.

Faking optimism
is a form
of self abandonment.
Dismissing it
altogether
is abusive.

Mistakes will happen.
Overdoses will happen.
An overdosed mind
is a mind
without sugar.
A mind unable
to think
the old
thoughts.

Mistakes
have the power
to usher in
new worlds.

Allow all the
banished
parts of you
a seat
at your table.

Gather
the sweetness
that needs
no measurement,
requires
no injection,
and pour it
generously
over
every
frightened
part
of
you.

Breathe, darling.
And again now.
Breathe.

Debee DiMenichi is a lover of many things…her husband of forty years, their three children and two grands. She loves collecting bones, breadcrumb trails, and clean sheets fresh off the clothesline. She is a way finder who helps her clients welcome all the banished parts of themselves to the table.

Bisbee, AZ, October 14, 2017
By Tia H. Ho

A Gift for You and the Healing of the World
By Fernanda Lodeiro

This world that is in pain, Mother Earth aching in every corner, her waters crying, sometimes shouting at us.

"How do we save this planet? How do we return to Eden?" you ask.

"Why is our health in trouble? Why are our lives in trouble?"

Because they are all a wake up call. An opportunity. A gift.

The way you can change the world is by changing first from within. From home, from the body, then we ripple. In our emotions, our mind, our whole field. In our communities and out into the world. With our actions, and our intentions.

You think you are a victim of this circumstance, this dis-ease. Remember, this is an opportunity.

"What does this have to do with Fertility?" you ask.

The Fertility journey has no defined outcome. It has no time. Yes, I hear you that it might feel like a curse. Yet, there is a gift. Not knowing when, or even if, you are left with the option of embracing the journey. A journey to ask, investigate, research, remember, clear, clean, detox, seek, reinvent, create. Heal. Everything. Including our deepest shit. A journey to return to wholeness.

Wholeness is not something that comes with a baby. It's our nature. And somehow, somewhere during our life we forget. Such is Fertility. A journey to reclaim Fertility (as many other journeys) is a journey to our wholeness, to our belonging, to Oneness.

Imagine that feeling, that sense of union, creative potential, pure love. Can you feel it? Exhilarating? Peaceful? Humbling? Love in its highest expression?

Joy.

The healing of the world that we are all hoping for requires beings that can bring immense creativity, love, and devotion. Light workers. Love workers. Could you imagine a better place to nurture them than in a nest that has remembered Wholeness?

The children you are calling in are waiting. They are many, many, many... Wise, old, highly evolved Souls, patiently awaiting our return home, to

Wholeness. That's how loving they are.

Fertility issues, like many other challenging conditions in this human form, can be a gift. A path to the healing of the world. Starting with your own. Would you be willing to embrace it? Would you be willing to open up and make your contribution? As much as you wish you could fight and avoid this journey, it all begins with surrendering to it.

Maybe the gift is only given to those who can unwrap it.

Fernanda Lodeiro, PhD, is a Whole Fertile Life and Feminine Leadership coach and the Soul midwife for incoming children. Trained as a biochemist and holistic health and life coach, Fernanda focuses on improving mind-body-spirit wellbeing in preparation for "baby calling" and parenting. She also supports women as they reclaim their creative power. "Nourishing the roots so life can unfold" is her mantra.
www.FernandaLodeiro.com

All Things Shall Be Revealed...
By Dawn Van Dyck

Looking back... the data points were there...it just took a while to connect all the dots that led you to this life. Those dots...some like shining stars in the night...stand out now, like signals marking the way. That night you lay in bed... wondering if you would go to your grave without anyone knowing the "real" you in your full expression. That was the opening that let me know you were ready...whether you knew it or not...to start down the path you were destined to walk. All the unplanned, unbelievable turns that got you here could never have been scripted as well. You've come so far...and by stepping into your truth the way that you did...you have shown yourself and others what is possible. Some have embraced it and learned...others may never see the gift that is there for them in what you have demonstrated. But that is their gift to unwrap...or not. Known misery? Or unknown joy??

So perhaps you thought that was it...that was your big plot twist...but that was just one of the key pieces of the puzzle to get you ready. Now that you've learned so much and are seeing the impact and import of how far you have come...now the real fun begins! Your Mama said you had a gift that you need to share...for yourself and all those whom your light shines upon. She named you "Dawn of a New Idea" for a reason! I've just needed to get you to the point where you can shed the beliefs that would hold you back and down...that would keep you from making YOU the priority. What you are learning now is just the beginning...but you're doing it. I can see that. And I know you can see and feel it, too. What you are doing...who you are being...bit by bit...is making a difference. Trust. Trust. Trust. And stay the course. I will be with you every step of the way, keeping you safe, guiding you through, and always, always loving you.

Dawn Van Dyck is a long time writer wannabe, living in Vermont, who has finally realized that to be a writer...all she needs to do is WRITE!! She has been writing for herself for a while now...and slowly but surely, she is finding her voice and gathering the courage and confidence to share her story. She is most grateful to be part of this loving, supportive community of writers.

Maybe

this is what it could be like

if you could learn to trust

and let life in.

By Amanda Chudak

Verve
By Melissa Pratt

Dear Crazee Hair Mom,

I'm a programmer at Verve. I wasn't sure whether to write a note to you, but
your low Joy Score for Verve caused me to take a look at how you play the game.

I'll give you this. You are a tenaciously hard player. Every day you play hard. But
your character always plays the game the same way every time, which causes
you to lose Verve. I know that you chase after Artifacts with great energy and
I can imagine your frustration when you catch one and it flies into the Abyss
every time you try to put it into the Vault. Here's the rule: You are only able to
have a certain number of Artifacts in your Vault. Again, you're holding on too
tightly to what you *think* you need.

By not resetting Verve you play with the same Artifacts every time you log on,
which causes the same results day after day. A different mix of Artifacts would
elevate your score and level you up to a new world. Could you maybe try
signing off and hit the reset button? When that Vault opens up you'll see what
happens. Crazy things can come together to do some amazing things. It's kind
of hard to predict it from where you are. Sometimes you just have to *trust* that it
will happen.

Also, you are trying to save everyone in the game, so every day you Drown,
Jump Off of a Cliff, Get Lost at Sea, and Run with Scissors. No one else does
that. They just try to save themselves. I can give you a hint. Most of those
things will send you to the bottom each and every time. You just can't win the
game by *trying* to save everyone else.

You know, we don't typically have low Joy Scores so I'm hoping that you're open
to trying some new things with Verve. I'm confident that if you are open to
playing the game in a new way you can live a life full of Verve.

Play on,
Jake

*Crazee Hair Mom is trying to get back to something that I loved in my teenage yeras—
writing! Just trying to find my bliss again, instead of playing life the same way over
and over again.*

In the Game Operators' Lunch Room
By Sylke Laine

Scene: Game Operators' lunch room

Game Operator 1: "Why the hell does she keep ignoring this knot in her stomach? I am constantly increasing the intensity, but she just will not pay attention to it!"

Game Operator 2: "Well, we had increased her tolerance for pain in the earlier levels, and..."

GOp 1: "But that was only for emotional pain. That's why I am giving her a physical sensation now!"

GOp 2: "Dude, we talked about this. Since version Sylke 4.0 they have been the same. Remember when she earned the Spiritual Awakening Badge in the Bottom of the Abyss Level? She learned to feel her emotions with her body, or whatever."

GOp 1: "Riiiiight, that night when she started bending the rules. I think I was on vacation, that's why I keep forgetting."

GOp 2 [*grabbing an energy drink from the fridge and mumbling to himself*]: "Drunk is what you were. Like half the time and that's why this game has gotten so confusing..."

GOp 1: "What?"

GOp 2: "Nothing!"

GOp 1: "So, still, if she is supposed to be so [*forming ironic quotation marks with his fingers*] 'in touch with her body and soul' then why won't she do anything about the knot? Makes no sense!"

GOp 2: "What's her denial status?"

GOp 1: "It's been so low recently that I hadn't even checked. Wait a second..." [*checks the game dashboard on his phone*]

GOp 2: [*sigh*]

GOp 1: "Man, it's way up there! How did that happen? She has it all wrong! That's like Princess Peach driving the opposite direction in Mario Kart!"

GOp 2: "It happens. They think it's a cheat. Or an easy way out."

GOp 1: "So what should I do? Do I need to set her back to the Abyss Level?"

GOp 2: "Noooo! Are you crazy? That would be way too harsh. Remember, she almost quit the game back then. Let's see. What are you even trying to tell her with the knot in her stomach?"

GOp 1: "Well, she needs to get more prayer and meditation in to boost her serenity status. She needs to get that up for the levels ahead."

GOp 2: "Hmm. Well, she has signed up for that writing class, hasn't she?"

GOp 1 [*checking dashboard again*]: "Sure has."

GOp 2: "Well, that gets her a self-care bonus. Maybe we could give her an assignment to trigger inward reflection?"

GOp 1: "It has worked before. Think she'll get it?"

GOp 2: "Let's also send her an invitation for tonight from her Yoga teacher. That should do it."

Operators high-fiving, leaving the lunch room, pleased with themselves.

I sometimes write. It mostly happens when the game operators are on lunch break and the fake news spreader in my head has been put on leave again for emotional harassment. You can reach me at sylke.laine@gmail.com and @mrslaine on Instagram.

From Behind the Veil
By Diane Roberson Douiyssi

Shoof, habibi! Look, my love!
Under all those layers,
there's you!

If you slow down and lean forward,
can you hear a call to prayer in the desert breeze?
It's your soul awakening unto itself.

Brush away the sands of sadness, my love,
masked as disregard.
You've let them drift in and cover your feet.

Gently sweep aside the veil of your inattention.
You'll find a strand of silver filigree
that graces your neck and adorns your words.

Fill the cups just once more with everyone else's expectations.
Then take your glass of tea, *habibi.*
Let its warmth burn your fingers as you feel your own desires.

Set down the tray laden with your past.
You don't need it anymore, my love.
Do you see how much lighter it feels?

Lift the hem of your dress, *habibi,*
and take a step past the fear that keeps you small like a secret.
Do you hear the lute calling?

Aji, habibi. Come, my love.
Step closer now, into the light of the fire.
Come dance to the music in your heart, and shine.

Diane is a writer, a writing mentor and a certified Martha Beck Life Coach at Inner Wisdom Wayfinding. She loves working with writers to tap into their deep inner wisdom, helping them bring their beautiful words into the world and live the lives they were meant to live.

RECOGNITION

Excited to See You
By Rebecca Liu

Pull back the curtain, slowly
You were not used to being open.
Ripened fruits hanging loose
Ready to be folded
Into steady, gentle palms.
But pause.
Let your skin drink
And bathe, in the cool air.

Dust particles of kisses
Wake up the hills and tickle
All that's been coiled deep
Inside your caves and valleys.

Space holds you up with pride,
Stars blink at the sight of you:
Long time no see.
The walls see you front and back,
They respond to every inch of your wilderness
With quiet companionship.

Let nothing but the air touch you,
Invisibly caressing you,
Softer than a feather.
Did you know you're a shore
Of lapping pleasure
Splashing glitter into the sky.

No one needs to understand
No one needs to know
How you fine tune yourself
To pick up the melody
Of every ripple
To play the beat
Of your vibrations
Into the song you knew you know.

See how your heart flutters
Even when no one's around.
Come back often.
We're excited to see you.

Rebecca Liu, Hong Kong & Seattle, WA. <u>www.rebeccaliu.net</u>

I Am Joan of Arc
By Laurel Morales

The baby wants to stay.
She wants to do backflips in this tiny red sea forever.

But Mama is losing blood, oxygen, sight.
Her mantra, "Can't, can't, won't."
The window, an invitation.

She plunges deep into an ocean of lies.
Fang tooth and wolf fish, vampire and viper squid.
Pale and molting, they sing a chorus:
"He never loved you. He never wanted you.
He doesn't even think about you."

"Can't, can't, won't."

Joan of Arc breaks through on the bullhorn:
You get to say 'can't' only one more time, Laurel.

"Ca…"

Joan clangs into the room, oranges stuck to her sword,
Reaches into the inky pool to yank Mama out into the light.

Time to push.
But first, do this one thing.

"What? Anything," Mama says.

Love yourself. That's all.
Because I am you. And I'm tired of this bullshit.

"You are me?"

Sapho and Sojourner, Susan and Mary,
We are all you.
And we are her.
And she is watching and she is keen.

"I am Joan.
I am revolution.
I am truth.
I am love.
I am.
And she is."

That's right. Now push.

When she's not writing, Laurel Morales spends her time as a mom of two girls, Scarlett and Lucia, and as a public radio reporter for Fronteras and NPR. She and her family live in Flagstaff, Arizona, where there is no shortage of inspiration—fiction and non.

Confessions of a Fake News Manufacturer
By Anisha Imhasly

OK, I'll admit it, it's been me all along. Fabricating those stories. Feeding the networks with a steady stream of fake news.

You can't imagine how easy it is! They'll believe just about anything if you just repeat it often enough. Very soon, it becomes real to them and then you manufacture the next story, and then the next. The thing is, these stories are appealing. They offer easy explanations.

So here's how these stories work. Shhhh…. I'll let you in on our industry secret! They have to feature an "I" and a "you," or an "us" and a "them." Other key ingredients are "right" or "wrong," and "good" or "evil." Other ingredients we like to add are shame and fear. Fear is basically in the DNA of all these stories.

These ingredients guarantee high-performance stories with a long life.

For stories to work and to be credible, they also have to involve a past and a future. Stories can't exist in the present alone. I mean, what do you even *do* with the present? Just sit there and look at a tree? Watch the paint dry? I mean, where's the *drama?*

Anyway, back to our fake news assembly line. Well, recently there's been a hitch. These rude, pesky journalists have been asking all these questions about our stories, like, "Is it true?" Outrageous! They're accusing us of not telling the truth, of fabricating evidence! I mean, between you and me, we *do* fabricate these stories, but that's an internal government secret!

It just makes us so mad. The Boss especially! He's been hovering around us like a predatory troll. (You don't know what a troll is? It's this animal from the cretinaceous *tyrannosaurus twitteri* family.) It's been a really challenging time for us, and you can be damn sure we're doing our best to defend against it. We've got a defense A-Team working for us.

I mean—how else are we going to keep this manufacturing unit, and the nation, safe? After all, we want To Be Great Again!

Although, let me tell you, I've been getting a little fed up around here lately. *Don't tell anybody I told you this.* You see, the stories we produce here, well, they get a little repetitive after a while. Don't get me wrong, I really believed them myself at first and all, but to be perfectly honest, they *are* a bit simple.

I don't really like what it's done to us as a company, or as a nation. It's divided a lot of people and some don't even talk to each other anymore. The stories give people satisfaction at first—a bit like getting a sugar rush—and then leaves them isolated and yearning for yet another story, and so on. Because, who would we be without our story, right?

I hope they never find out I told you this because I'd lose my job here at EGO NEWS CORP, Ltd.

It's been really nice talking with you!

Anisha Imhasly was born in Bombay, India, and lives in Bern, Switzerland, where she runs a coaching practice. Her heart stretches across continents to contain the multitudes of scattered family diaspora and kindred spirits.

Entropy and Evolution in One
By Tia H. Ho

She thought she was falling apart.
That the years of building a life
on partial, borrowed truths
handed to her from a reliably unwell mind,
that this fraction of stability
meant she was only marginally real.

**

A pinhole view
in the doorway
had let her see inside.

**

She thought she was falling apart
as each small piece of old lie,
the forced pieces of her,
fell away,
as sand into a pile.

**

The pinhole widened,
expanded in the doorway,
opening to a panorama view.

**

She thought she was falling apart.
That if any of the positives she had created
out of the dust of childhood
also dropped into the pile...
what would be left?

**

She thought she was falling apart,

so she let go

as the storm of someone else's lies,
complete in their untruth,
tore through in a gale force wind —

scattering each grain of sand.

**

The pinhole...

the door...

disappeared,

leaving only vistas as far as she could see,

all of the world inside.

As a child Tia was a tree climber, insect finder, and lover of living things. Now she is an author, a community health strategy diviner, and an explorer of wonder. She has a few fancy degrees, which she uses to help others displace fear by building love through collaborative endeavors.

Cape Tribulation, Queensland
By Judith Stewart

Beauty Within the Beast
By Sandi Means

Abandoned, isolated and lost in the enfolding darkness the beast sits caged.
She howls and moans at the bars that separate her from life.
Days go by, and the beast fills with despair, shame and a longing to be free.

Despair turns to rage.
She rattles and shakes the barricade to no avail.
Losing all hope of freedom, she retreats.

Suddenly light fills the cage. Love holds up a mirror to the Beast.
She turns away, her face pressed against the bars.
Love reaches through and taps her shoulder. "Look!"

"No longer a beast — is that beauty me?
She looks so free. She cannot be my reality."
Love says, "The mirror shows the love that lies within."

"Love?" The beast shrugs. "Maybe. Yet in this cage I remain."
Love answers, "Look around. You'll find the key."
There it is, glimmering in the light. The key!

Gathering her last shards of courage, the beast turns the key.
The lock pops open. Love beckons her forward.
She is free.

Love whispers, "You always had the key.
You put yourself in the cage.
The love and beauty within you needed to see."

The beast — now Beauty revealed — looks at her cage.
"Where do I go from here?" she asks. Silence.
"Love! Where have you gone?" she wails.

"Open your heart. I am always here," Love whispers.
"See your own light within you, and you will see light without."
"Pfft. You speak in riddles. Just look around — it's dark." Beauty replies.

Silence falls. Beauty rages. "You did this to me! This darkness is your making!
You left me. How can I see beauty with no light?"
"Open my heart." She mumbles. "How do I do that?"

"It's not my fault!" she bellows. "They put me there within those bars!"
She slumps to the floor, her head on her knees.
Love answers, "Are you ready to listen now my dear?"

Beauty lifts her head and shrugs.
Love smiles. "Listen to your heart beat. Relax and focus on that love within."
Beauty sighs. Then sighs again. "Wait. I feel it." She places her hand on her chest.

Love replies, "Open your eyes. Fear has kept them closed. Look around you."
"How did I not see this before? The stars. The moon. It takes my breath away," Beauty says.
"You had to look to see," Love answers.

Beauty sighs. "Another of your riddles!"
"To see beauty outside, you have to look with your heart."
Beauty sits in silence. "How do I listen to my heart?"

Love smiles. "My dear, just ask yourself which choice brings you joy."
Beauty smiles. "Within my heart are my answers." Then she leaps up.
"Look! A path has opened before me. My heart has found the way!"

The Reluctant Genie
By Katja Svensson

There she goes again, smiling and saying she is fine. Her good girl face cracks by a fraction and the smoke coming from her lava of anger and frustration seeps out just a little.

She feels deeply guilty that she does not love her life. She has chosen most of her circumstances after all. There is so much to be grateful for, so why is she not happy? Does that make her insatiable? Ungrateful? Perhaps lacking in sense and judgment?

Her Guardian Angel—who has shown great patience with this stubborn one— sighs.

Does she not know she is her own genie? The power to manifest rests at her finger tips. Limitless wonders, ready to be evoked. She can create and recreate her world as many times as she desires. No need to feel beholden to choices of the past.

The Angel smiles at the thought of some of the more colourful life choices and marvels at how beautiful her life tapestry has become.

If only she could see it.

Katja's bio is in flux as she is in the process of shaping her next adventure. She is hopeful it will include lots of passionate cooking, some heartfelt writing and a return to Africa. She currently resides in Barbados with her beautiful daughter.

Confessions of a Flight Risk
By Danielle E. Fournier

I love men.

So much, in fact, that I have never really stopped to look at one for longer than it takes to assess his possibility as a soul mate (perhaps), his probability as a good kisser (most likely) and, *egad*...his potential net worth (ever increasing).

It might seem shocking that a woman who has had her heart broken so many times would be a heartbreaker, even if simply out of decency, but no, I can filet a soul like a salmon on Sunday.

Not just the "nice guys" or the "meh, he really likes sports guys" but also the "OMG, didn't know that kind of sex was possible guys" or the "wow, no one has ever made me breakfast before AND likes my ill mannered dog guys."

I, simply, no longer can commit.

To my destruction. My undoing.

My grief over losing the one man I really loved.

Imagine my horrific surprise when I was ghosted by a hot pilot I picked up on a trip to Maui last fall.

Seems like I should have seen it coming.

Brilliant and analytical with a wicked sense of humor. He bragged over his children endlessly while politely sipping his drink as I downed vodka to let loose.

Despite the red flags, I pressed on. After all, we had so much in common.

He objected to my age (13 years younger), extolled the joys of being single (fishing with guys, hunting with guys, hanging with the guys), and told me a very precise and rehearsed version of why he would never, ever marry again.

I fancy myself a romantic, so I suggested more sake and sushi.

We stumbled along the street (me from alcohol and him from an injury), where I pulled him aside for a kiss that sank deep into my soul.

Kissing ability: *Check*. Net worth potential: *Check*. Soul mate possibility: *Check*.

My memory of the dinner is a blur, but I know that he stood up over the table and kissed me in front of everyone. As though he was checking to see if it was as good as the first one. A sure sign.

The night passed and you can easily guess the rest.

Drunk girl+airline pilot=steamy bedroom and awkward moments.

Moments like, "Well, I am good for another six years" and, "Um, we should travel!" and "No, we should digest this..." (awkward hug).

Too many phone calls and too many texts later...

"You need dynamite to break me down."

But...*you already let me in!*

Radio Silence. Ad nauseam. Add wine. Add everyone is sick of hearing it.

But, oh, *it hurts...how could he?*

I let a possibility in. A hope. A moment of rapture spent in another's presence. Talking. Laughing. Exchanging stories of water.

Many months later, I think of how badly I hurt. And not over
Mr. Two divorces-professional cheater wives-and five kids-crossing the oceans-ensuring the safety of hundreds of passengers-everyday.

Oh.

It hurts. *I* hurt. Oh. Oh.

Oh.

Danielle E. Fournier is an author and coach specializing in a spiritual approach to creativity. Visit her website at <u>www.daniellefournier.com</u>.

Satanic Airlines Flight 666 to Hell
By Emma Campbell Webster

Hello, and welcome aboard this Satanic Airlines flight 666 to Hell. Please listen carefully to the following announcement.

Shortly after take-off, the flight crew will pass through the cabin offering complimentary snacks, beverages, university degrees, and creatively fulfilling jobs that provide you with a reasonable income and a respectable place in society. After reaching cruising altitude, we will hit a pocket of turbulence so severe it will cause total engine failure and we will immediately begin a terrifying nose-dive towards certain death. Your nearest emergency exits are nine years ahead of you, your oxygen mask is broken, and your life vest is full of holes. At this point, you may wish to read the copies of Eckhart Tolle's *A New Earth* and *The Power of Now* provided in the seat pocket in front of you.

As we make our descent, the force generated by our velocity will simultaneously burn up your old identity, most of your relationships, and any semblance of an identifiable role in normal society. As you finally come to terms with the inevitability of your own death, the plane will crash into the mountainside and break into a million pieces.

Miraculously, you will survive.

When you come to, you will have no idea who you are. At first, you will be forced to survive by barbecuing the remains of your fellow passengers. It will be grim, but you'll find some mini sachets of ketchup in the plane's wreckage and eventually you'll be able to convince yourself that it tastes just like chicken. For the first few days you will waste what little energy you have trying to attract the attention of potential rescuers, before eventually realizing that nobody whatsoever is coming to save you, not even your own mum. For a while you will sink into despair, and get as drunk as you can on the few miniature bottles of whisky you are able to find scattered across the mountainside. Once those have run out, you will mope around the mountain feeling sorry for yourself, wishing you'd taken a different flight, and wondering what all the people who took different flights are doing, and how much better your life would be if only you'd taken one. And then, eventually, you will get so tired of yourself that you will go for a walk instead. While walking, you will find a small notebook, and you will take that, along with the Satanic Airlines pen you found in the coat pocket of yesterday's lunch, and you will start writing a journal. In it, you will pour your anger, grief, despair, fear, hope, curiosity, and love. You will pour out the entire contents of your head and heart, from the blackest, to the most sublime, until there is *absolutely nothing left*.

At that moment, you will become aware of a still, empty space of peace, and you will have found what you have been looking for your whole life: your true self.

And then, my love, we will talk.

Emma Campbell Webster is a writer and performer. She is the author of <u>*Lost in Austen,*</u> <u>*Create Your Own Jane Austen Adventure*</u> *and publishes on* <u>Medium.com</u>. *Originally from England, she now lives in Los Angeles with her husband and two daughters.*

Prayer
By Anna Smith

My mother says, *I'll hold you in the light.* She's Quaker, and prefers this to the more southern, *I'll pray for you,* with its shade of just how damned you are.

But sometimes—this holding in the light—it brings to mind a certain hand: King Kong's, and the tiny, screaming blonde in the clingy white dress. He loves her so much, but doesn't know how to say it. And his hand is just so big.

Searchlights sweep and cross. She's terrified, but finally gets it. Even the crowd sees and falls silent.

It loves her, it won't hurt her. The light is a friend.

Anna Smith is a writer, teacher, and creativity coach. She grew up in North Carolina, and now lives on a small farm in Massachusetts.

Floating Upwards, Borobudur
By Naina Saligram

Garden of the Parallels
By Corry Angwar

I came to sit in the garden,
amongst the devotees and the monk,
feeling like an odd shaped statue.
Everyone was looking but trying not to look
to figure out what shape I would turn to be:
a rogue?
an adversary?
a curious non believer?

I let them talk
while I observed my surrounding.
It was a small garden,
with a few tall trees,
their canopies hung low,
giving shade of coolness on a summer's day.
Greeneries, blue skies, and sunshine just like any other day,
but one blink is all it takes.
Now seeing outside, inside
a pool of clarity in my heart
an endless tunnel of light
a void of emptiness, brightness
simultaneously crashing
with darkness,
a parallel world
of black and white.

The light lit up my soul,
unfazed by the presence of sorrow
simply noticing its shadow sister.
The light carries me up,
floating amongst the clouds
like an air balloon catching a ride from the wind.

I found contained within myself
A Greater Universe.

Student of Life. Kid at Heart. Introvert and Ultimate Cave Woman. Part Poet, Part Florist, Part Therapist, Part Artist. Food Enthusiast. Lazy Cook. Occasional Baker. Nature Lover. Find her poetry @ medium.com/@corry.ang, her blog @ lupuscarecommunity.wordpress.com/.

Esker
By Tricia Elliott

Yes, I have language.
I know things.
I hypothesize and methodize and conclude from our results
that more questions will follow,
just like you.

But this.
This I cannot randomize or control.
I don't think it can be replicated. I don't know.
What I do know is that we are

Tectonic.
Geologic.
Glacial in our sway.

We are masquerading mountains
with seismic beating hearts.
Magma pulses in our marrow,
bore tides rush along our spines.

It was night.
"Move your earth self," murmured
the wind, stirring the hemlocks with
feathered beak and whiskered tail,
leading with furred footpads past bleached river bones.
I followed
as the rocks quaked in ganglia
and stretched in starry veins,
ice sprouting tarn and kettle.
All of it a wordless, rooted exchange.
All of it a needled shimmer humming
home to the self,
a cirque shell left behind.

I can't prove this happened.
But I believe in
the moraine of this body,
this sentimental sediment
of elemental respiration,
no longer solid, but light

being lived,
being breathed,
being moved.

We are living fossils.
We are the esker, the snaking glacial river.
We can shed these illusions of
boundaries.
We can erode this evidence
of form.

Tricia delights in exploring the woods and mountains of Alaska with her dogs, snuggling in the yurt with her two daughters (and dogs), and channeling her inner mystic poet among fellow writers.

Flying With My Father
By Usha Rani Sharma

Daddy-ji said to anyone who was listening
That England is a *mithi* jail, a sweet prison.
Yes, we have flushing toilets, central heating,
Hot and cold, clean water in plenty,
All the material comforts we did not have in Dhin Pur, India,
But my spirit longs for the wide open endless fields
Trimmed by the light. Where is the temple bell?
Where is the *triveni sangam*, holy confluence of three trees
That sanctifies the village? The *peepal*, the *neem*, and the *bodhi* trees twining
Around each other and growing as one, healing and shading all with impartial
love.

I absorbed his longing into my cells,
My own imprisoned cages of lack,
Lived in collusion with the collective in my well-defended cocoon,
Manufactured by our shared yearning to soar.
For years, I toiled inside the cocoon of conditioning,
Disguising myself in smart polyester trousers as a competent woman of the
world.
Until one day, the wild *sadhu* in me awoke and cried out,
Recognized the *triveni sangam*, the holy trinity in myself and everyone.
The three sacred rivers, Ganga, Yamuna and invisible Saraswati
Merge in our shining forehead, oh Yes,
Flowing from the ground of all existence, *satchitananda*.
I emerge with wet and gentle untangle of butterfly wings
And tell the truth so that we fly: Free.
The temple bell resounds
Through the light of my words.

Usha R. Sharma lives in Silicon Valley (aka The Valley of Heart's Delight), USA.

ACCEPTANCE

How I Frack Myself
By Mia Brown

I rage in indignation:
"Is nothing sacred to you?!
Do you not see how precious the land is?
Are you really so callous that
the pained faces of the people have no effect on you?"

And then I see.
I see why I feel it deep in my body.
It is not just the land,
I, too, am fractured.

Sweet body, I have harmed you.
I gave you to those who had not earned the right to enter.
Ignored your signals of distress.
Refused to give you nourishment.
Turned your worth over to the unwise.
Worked you to depletion.
Shamed your feminine.
Tamed your wild.
Gave your gems away for cheap.

Please forgive me.
How do I make amends?

The answer comes with the smoothness of silk.
"With ease you cherish the undulating field.
You must find a way to do the same with the slopes of your body."

And so I look at its nakedness for longer than is comfortable. The marks on my
thighs like shallow canyons, formed by the stretching of land as it breathes and
grows with life. I can glimpse the beauty.
My hair unruly, like the reaching of branches towards sunlight twisting in
asymmetry.
Let the beauty in.
My shoulders, delicate, and muscles lean. Consciousness chose this form, I
remind myself.
I glimpse a softness of spirit in my eyes, doe's eyes, listening, feeling, noticing.
I'm trying.

I see I must offer myself the tenderness that I implore of you when you see
the earth as just a commodity. My currency may be approval, love, control, but
the energy is the same — of exploitation, lack of reverence for the mysteries
within.

My fearful animal worries you will win.
You destroy so casually and you have the values of a society lulling you into
trance — consumption, materialism, power. Sirens singing songs of not enough.
But when I listen to the earth, it is also the part of myself that no longer wants
to cause self-destruction.
Then I feel the weight of true power.
Do you feel it?
Do you feel how you also fracture yourself, when you fracture the earth?
How you fracture the earth when you fracture yourself?
They cannot be unwoven.

It pains me to watch you silence the voices of the people who have loved the
land for ages.
Oh, I see.
Where have I silenced myself?
Where have I snuffed out the sacred?
It is time that I speak from my roots, grounded in a truth older than my body.
The wise woman within, who has lifetimes of knowledge of what it means to be
feminine, what it means to be human, is ready to share her story of wholeness.
I yearn to listen, to become a student of integrity.
And for you, I wish the same.
I wish for the great mother to take up her thread and reweave the holes within
and without and between.
I wish for the surrender — to let her.

Ignoring the Stubble
By Leah Carey

"Don't touch me there," she said. "I haven't shaved."

I didn't care if she had shaved — I just wanted to touch her.

"Don't look down there," she said. "It's ugly."

I wanted to spend hours gazing at her magnificence, at her "down there."

"Don't tell me I'm beautiful," she said. "I know I'm fat."

The fact that her body had borne and nourished two children didn't make her "fat" — it made her strong, mature, wise, and stunningly gorgeous.

I wanted to stare, to touch, to revel, to FEAST on every inch of her body. But she could only accept pleasure in the dark, under the covers, hidden away.

I felt rejected when I told her how beautiful she was and she dismissed my words with a wave of her hand, a shake of her head.

And I thought back...

To all the times I had said, "No. I haven't shaved."

"I'm ugly."

"I'm fat."

To those I turned away because I had a jiggle.

To the lovers I rejected because I didn't feel worthy of their attention.

To the exclamations over my beauty that I dismissed as the ravings of lunatics.

Now I've been to the other side of the mountain.

I am the one who has been turned away because another couldn't understand that her beauty radiated out of every pore. She couldn't understand that she was, quite possibly, the most alluring woman I had ever seen. That I wanted so much more of her body, while she wanted to give me less.

How often have they wanted more of me while I shrank into the shadows?

Yes, I jiggle. Yes, I worry about how I look, smell, taste, feel. I assume that I will be judged in every moment, from every angle.

But now I wonder — am I the one doing most of the judging?

Because you know what I've never heard anyone say?

"Never mind. Put your clothes back on."

They seem no more concerned about my jiggle than I was about hers.

Whether her underarms were stubbly was of no importance when there were so many wonders to concentrate on.

And if they find my "down there" half as fascinating as I found hers, what more could I ask?

I wish she could see her body the way I did. But since she doesn't, I will send out this silent blessing...

Thank you. In showing me what it looks like to not appreciate your magnificent body, you've shown me what a gift it would be to appreciate my own.

Originally published at www.soulspring.org.

Leah Carey is a real-life storyteller. Whether she's telling other people's stories in her work as a journalist, or helping people tell their own stories in writing and onstage, she is dedicated to helping us understand ourselves and each other through the stories of everyday life. Find her at www.LeahCarey.com.

Ode to Old Lady Arm
By E. B. Brown

Well-traveled,
Jiggling wonton —
You suddenly appear,
When I feign a coquettish gesture,
Flirting with
My last hope to charm
And feel
Like a loved beauty
From an era I never knew
Even when I lived there.

There's a faint odor, too,
A bitterness, a sour taste,
That makes the wriggling, snow-white
Yet no-longer-baby flesh
Appear to be
A prunier testament,
Greater than
The truth of my birth certificate.

I can't run away from you
Anymore.
So, I wiggle you in the mirroring afternoon sunlight,
Knowing
There's so much more road to cover,
With very little time.
Still,
I am smiling,
I know we've already crossed the roads —

For there, right there, in that Old Lady Arm,
The ribbons of our travels home,
Float free,
Unperturbed.

Purposepreneur Creative, Lee Collver-Richards (pen-name E. B. Brown), delights when courageous practices emerge out of tender collaborative care. A professionally certified Transformational Learning Practitioner (M.Ed.), Lee aspires to create by heart the kinds of compassionate structures that promote the building of clean, happy, healthy, prosperous environments in every community on Earth.

Wild
By Annelie Ferreira

I knew about the scar long before I could see it.

Siblings can always be relied on to point out any oddities in you they were lucky enough to be spared.

But it was only when I wanted the yellow swimsuit that I finally understood what the scar meant.

"Not that one," my mother said. "It is cut too low at the back, it will show the mark at the bottom of your spine. It was not like a normal growth the doctors took off when you were born, you know. It was more like a . . . small tail. Never let people see it."

Next I learnt the truth about my ears.

I wanted to grow my hair longer than the bob my mother always cut for me.

My sister said, "Are you serious? You would need to tie back your hair in a ponytail like mine, and then people will see your ears. You know they are too big, don't you? As it is they stick out through your bob sometimes, you really should take more care."

Nails were a consistent problem. My father said he'd never seen a child with such dirty fingernails, that's what happened when you played outside too much.

My mother solved the problem by clipping them to the quick regularly. For days after each clipping my fingers would feel numb and stupid.

But the worst was the day my mother took me to the doctor because the PT teacher sent her a note.

"I can't believe it," the doctor said, peering at the scaly patch on my chest through his magnifying glass. "I have never seen this on a human. It is common in dogs, though."

I remembered my granddad. Once when he watched me eat, his eyes sparkled as he said, "When you have finished with a bone, kid, it is so clean not even a dog would look at it."

At the time I felt proud.

Now I realised I should have been ashamed of it.

I stopped eating meat.

Soon after that I became pale, and ill. It was a strange kind of illness. I would faint for no reason, or my stomach ached relentlessly, or weeping sores broke out on my arms. Once I got a scratch round my ankle that became infected. My brother said it looked disgusting, like I had stepped into a wolf trap.

I limped from day to day.

Then, one day, a terrible storm came up. We were sent home from school immediately, to get to safety as quickly as possible.

I lagged behind the others.

Then I stopped. I didn't know why, but I turned back. I turned towards the storm.

I battled against the wind past one house, two houses, three. I had just crossed a street when it happened. A huge tree smashed down right in front of me. I had no time to jump away before a branch struck me, knocking me out cold.

When I came to, a man was bending over me. I caught a glimpse of beads under his shirt. When he spoke, it was with a strange accent.

"How are you feeling?" he asked.

"I'm fine," I said. "It's just that . . ."

I started crying. I couldn't stop myself. Everything spilled out, about the fainting, and the horrible sores, and how I ached so much sometimes.

The man sat down next to me. The wind had died down completely, it was strange.

When the man spoke again, I noticed for the first time that he had my granddad's eyes.

"Were you by any chance born with a tail?" he asked.

Annelie Ferreira is an award-winning author and artist from South Africa, currently living in the UK. She believes in magic, that we can be reborn at any age, and that there is an infinity of possibilities inside each of us.

How I Got Rid of my "Sure-I-Can-Do-That-For-You" Scarf and "You-Can-Rely-On-Me-For-Everything" Hat
By Kaliopi Nikitas

For years I dressed myself daily in a very predictable manner. I'd put on my "button-down-responsible-adult" shirt on top of my "dutiful-daughter-and-sister" pants and layer on my "prompt-responder-to-all-crises" vest. Before heading out the door I'd don my "going-above-and-beyond-anything-I-tackle" coat and, for good measure, I would take my "you-can-rely-on-me-for-every-thing" hat and "sure-I-can-do-that-for-you" scarf.

As the years went by and life became more complex, so too did my wardrobe. I began amassing new 'looks' as I took on more roles and responsibilities, adding outfit after outfit to my already overstuffed closet and drawers.

Initially, I didn't mind some of the tight, constricting clothes I had to wear. After all, my "exercise-until-you-fit-into-a-size-zero-or-else-you're-fat" pantyhose and my "work-hard-every-second-of-your-life-to-prove-yourself" dress resulted in oh so many compliments. Who doesn't like being admired? And as others' admiration and respect for me grew, the more I measured my worth by the hats I wore and the sacrifices I made.

With time, the undergarments of "discipline-and-selflessness" and an "I-can-be-Wonder-Woman-and-gracious-at-the-same-time" bra began to pinch and become very uncomfortable. I could barely wait to get home to tear them off so I could breathe freely.

As my tolerance for self-inflicted pain and misery waned, a radical thought began to form...

"What if I peel off these layers of duty, expectation, and overachievement? What would be left?"

The internal dialogue that ensued lasted for years, with a devil and angel on each shoulder.

Then, like a flash of lightning, the truth illuminated the stormy landscape of my thoughts. The birth of my nephew ignited a spark of clarity.

With reverent awe, I marveled at this tiny wonder, the unfathomable miracle I held gingerly in my arms. This wee baby entered the world without any clothes or identities; in fact, he didn't even have a name. He didn't need a cloak of conformity to be pure preciousness. He just was.

As I imagined this sweet existence growing into adulthood, it was clear to me that his developmental metamorphosis would not in any way change the fact that he was a priceless being. Another luminous thunderbolt: the same holds true for me, and you, and every single human being on the planet.

So, what did I end up doing, you ask?

No, I did not become a nudist or shun all attire as a result of this realization.

I simply began to acknowledge my true nature prior to getting dressed everyday.

Now, I take a moment to nod to the fact that I am life manifested—that I am enough.

I do not need to define or justify my existence with the garbs of imposed identity;

I enter and exit this world in my skin, the garment of my soul.

Hello, my name is Kaliopi. I am a Life Coach and Mind-Body Coach. I help overwhelmed, people-pleasing, ultra-responsible women redirect their care and energy toward themselves so they can stop being everyone else's life-saver, and begin to "savour" their own life. My own personal journey of dealing with an autoimmune disease and radically changing my life has led me to where I am now: helping others transform illness and adversity into empowerment while living with authenticity, meaning and awe.

The Dirty Bathroom
By Blossom Lievore

Do you have a dirty bathroom? Because I have one. It's in a separate building, away from the house. You have to go outside to get there, even in the rain. It's made of plywood and doesn't have any windows. It has a washing machine and dryer, closet, cupboard, and our shower.

Everything is overflowing and holds more than it was designed to.

There are spiders and cobwebs and a naked light bulb that hangs from the ceiling.

Do you have a dirty bathroom? Because I have one. It's dark and filled with self-loathing, shame, and petty angry thoughts. In the corner are piles of bad decisions and loneliness.

Do you have a dirty toilet? Because mine just won't get clean. I've scrubbed it on my hands and knees with the most toxic substances you can imagine. Still, the stains will not get out, no matter how hard I try.

Do you have a dirty toilet? Because I have one I simply cannot get clean, that I've punished on my hands and knees. I scrub it with it with unhealthy decisions and poor life choices until it's raw. And still, there are vicious stains impossible to hide.

I have a dirty bathroom, it's cluttered, dingy, and dark. I would just like for it to be clean.

How can you clean a dirty bathroom that's undeserving of redemption or grace?

Well, I am going to try something new. I've heard people tell me what the secret is. I haven't tried it yet because I don't believe it works. It might have worked for them, but it won't work for me.

My bathroom is just too dirty and filled with unredeemable sins.

But, I'm going to try.

I'm going to try to love my bathroom.

Wise women, who know about such things, have said to just wash it with fresh water and soap. I'm also going to wash it with love and forgiveness.

I'm going to embrace the beautiful marks that tell the story of a life lived with passion.

I am going to sit on the floor in my bathroom and gently wash away the scuffs and the scars. I'm going to lovingly escort every spider out from every dark corner.

My bathroom is beautiful. It has water that runs both hot and cold.

If you are dirty, you can stand under the water and be washed clean.

Would you like to try it? It will work for you too.

I stumbled into Write into Light while reading and writing fanfiction for The Walking Dead. This is my first time writing for real.

The Truth Was Wary of Her
By Laura Harbin

The Truth was wary of Her.
Playmates as children, they danced, hop-scotched and double-dutched freely.
But She abandoned The Truth when her thirteen-year-old heart was broken,
And She told no one.

Reunions were thwarted.
Concealed in closets, The Truth bargained freedom through keyholes.
But She kept her back pressed to the doors.
The Truth could not be trusted to preserve the story.

The last clash was catastrophic.
Banished, The Truth became only a persistent, distant echo.
She chose Betrayal and Denial as her companions now.
Constantly with one or the other, never at peace.

Then The Truth exploded in an unrequited homecoming.
Betrayal and Denial called out, we are so glad you are here!
But She was not. It had been too long.
She did not recognize The Truth any longer.

She lay broken on the floor, wary of The Truth.
Freed from Siberian isolation, periodically breathing warmth onto her cheek,
The Truth paced next to Her, and waited.
Finally, She lifted her head up from the tiles, and reached out her hand.

The Truth embraced Her, now requited.
She asked The Truth if they were alone.
Brutal, Ugly, Sober, Bitter, Plain, Sad, Necessary, and Profound are all here.
And so is Divine.
That's You, She said.
They are all Me, The Truth said.
And they are all You.

Laura Harbin is a Springsteen-loving, hockey-playing vegetarian living and writing in Toronto, Canada. She has worked in film and television for over twenty years and recently transitioned from producing to writing. She is currently working on original television series ideas and watching television as research (!). Her twelve-year-old is jealous. And suspicious.

Total Solar Eclipse, August 21, 2017
By Susan A. Ring

The Golden Ticket
By Kim Smith

This is it.

There were no white flashes of light or great shifting in the cosmos or my immediate environment. NO-thing happened.

Only the message: *THIS IS IT.* I felt this truth in my bones, blood, and soles of my feet. Breathing was easier. BE-ing was.

Three words capable of holding as much beauty and hope for the experience of this vibrant life as is divinely possible. You being born and being alive is the coveted Golden Ticket.

OR three words containing a damning finality of a meager existence. Kind of like, I was expecting the Golden Ticket and all I got was this lousy T-shirt.

If I had been listening to God five years ago, drowning in alcoholism, self-hatred, and the bottomless cocktail of FearRageBlameShame, and THIS is the message I received, I would have told God, he/she/it could go fuck themselves.

I used to curse at God a lot. My life wasn't easy. And it was perfect. The fear. The anger. The blame. The shame. My insane mother. The seatbelt that saved my life and lacerated my liver. The millions of malignant mini monsters that wanted me dead and took up residence in my neck. Every blackout. Every misstep. It was all God. It was all perfect.

I think it's possible to fall in love with the parts of yourself that used to terrify you. In fact, I recommend it.

Today I'm listening more. Fear, rage, shame, and blame still play mini-roles in my life. They inflame themselves when I need to learn something, lately: that more love is always the answer. And, I need to point that love first at myself for it to have the greatest impact on others.

My mom is still unhinged. The polar caps are melting. The world is in chaos. Evil is alive. I've heard that EVIL spelled backwards is LIVE. That evil is the divine showing us how NOT to be. The absence of God shows us God's presence.

And I am not afraid. I see Consciousness working in all of it, the light and the shadow, in every action and event, God is everywhere. God is everyone.

If you woke up grumpy AF, lost your keys, watched Netflix all day and are still wearing the same yoga pants from yesterday, that's God choosing to be you as you.

If you woke up grateful AF, meditated, volunteered and are having the best hair day EVER, that's the Divine choosing to be you as you.

If you *remember* and handle life like a boss. That's Consciousness choosing to be you as you.

If you *forget* and handle life like a bratty child. That's Spirit choosing to be you as you.

You've won the Golden Ticket.

There is no wrong way to be you.

There is no right way to be you.

There is only Being, and you being you is enough.

When you live this way long enough, believing this to be true with awareness and presence, God no longer chooses to be you.

You realize you are Consciousness itself.

THIS IS IT

Kim Smith is a sober mama, writer, yogini, and mermaid. She hopes to change the world by sharing her voice and her experience. If you'd like to follow along on her journey of truth telling, she can be found on FB @therealkimsmith and on Instagram @thereal_kimsmith.

Enough
By Kat Soong

learned goals of greatness
internalized
the best
always striving to be better
do better

constant judgment spews forth unconsciously
masked as self-motivation
self-inflicted emotional assault ensues
verbal diarrhea at its best
it is the default
ingrained in the depths of my being
every cell vibrates with the tension of it
cultural
societal
gender specific

Not refined enough
Not good enough
Not pretty enough
Not skinny enough
Not smart enough
Not enough
Never enough

deafeningly loud
tracks on repeat
distorted reality
like mirrored reflections in a fun house
except this is not fun
it's damning and damaging

planting seeds
sharing lessons
desperate to believe
preaching
but not living the truth
my truth for others
but not for me

tortured and straining to be more

Stop.

see what they see
the Truth
unclouded reality

Just as I am.

Enough.
Completely Enough.
Complete and Enough.

Croning
By Jill Syme

From my vantage point as a crone,
Seeing clearly the seduction of a noble friend.
Bait and switch, sleight of hand, soul-baring candor.
Lo and behold, nemeses cloned from my DNA.
Their cruelty was my cruelty. Their abuse was my abuse.
I wish I'd known. So many wasted years of inner violence.

I was the perpetrator of self-abuse.
Outraged by **his** actions, a legacy of finger pointing in my DNA,
Pointing those same fingers at myself is true candor.
A glimmer of awareness arrives on a lightning bolt. A noble friend?
Oh, misspent youth, craving vengeance while inflicting violence.
Nowhere on the horizon was the wisdom of a crone.

Angry, clamoring for justice, I ignored the sweet whispers of the crone.
Instead, craving a megaphone to spread the word of his abuse.
Show up and shut up. That, too, was in my DNA.
Mixed messages from my mind and soul, so NOT friends.
Inner frenemies, akin to Sybil's alter egos, did not inspire candor
But stalked my better angels who counseled compassion, not violence.

Still I could not see my nemesis as a noble friend.
Hell, I was distracted, spouting self-righteous anger instead of soul-baring
candor.
"Him, him, him," was my battle cry. "End the abuse."
And then the voice of the crone
So clear and so wistfully she chirped, "Stop your inner violence.
Psychically remove it from your DNA."

I ask her, "What's a noble friend?"
A seeming adversary who reflects your inner violence,
Who mirrors your self-abuse,
And has agreed to be hated to spark your candor,
To highlight the unfinished business hidden in your DNA.
I query, "How do I become be a crone?"

"Compassionate witnessing and forgiveness," answered the crone.
"Extract the warrior's sword in your DNA.
He is you and you are he. That's candor.
Witness all that you marginalized, silenced, exiled in self-abuse.

Your evil twin was only trying to curb your inner violence.
He was your noble friend."

My crone is my shepherd; I shall not want for candor any longer.
Violence forgiven of self and noble friends.
Self-abuse gracefully cut from my DNA.

Jill Syme, Ph.D., is a certified Caroline Myss Archetypal Consultant, a Family Business Consultant specializing in relationships in family-owned business, and a ReVisioneer™ who helps people see their lives through different eyes.

Finding Freedom
By Tracey Hewitt

That box that people put you in, the pigeon hole which satisfies their need to classify and order their experiences, you don't quite fit, do you?

There's that sharp edge that grabs and catches. You try to smooth it off, sand it away, for your comfort — and for theirs.

Stop.

That sharp edge is your power. File it away and your unique shape is lost.

It's tempting to force yourself into that box shape.

To fit.

To fit in.

But, that sharp edge digs into your side and deep down you know this isn't the shape of you. It would not be this uncomfortable if it were.

Your place is not inside any box. No pigeon hole can contain your complexity, your contradictions, and the fullness of who you are.

That sharp edge? It's your reminder that you don't belong in any box, and it's your sword to cut yourself free.

Tracey lives with cowboys and listens to angels. She writes and paints, balances cash-books and manages logistics. Surrounded by her family and a menagerie of animals, she lives in the Aussie bush near a billabong. Her grandkids think she sings the best Incy-Wincy spider ever. Others may disagree. <u>traceyhewitt.com</u>

RECLAMATION

The Truth of You Does Not Need to Be Contained:
An Ode to Those with Rubbermaid Bins Stacked Neatly in the Closet
By Kate Godin

You are not too much. You are not.

I know the discipline it takes to keep from spilling out all over the place. I know that the careful organization of your emotions feels safe and looks good. But the truth of you does not need to be contained.

The ocean, too, would fear its vastness, its depths, its infinite shades of green-bluegray if it didn't know it was an ocean. Imagine the anxiety in that rippling body of life for trying—and failing—to gather itself into a plastic cup! But it is not the job of the ocean to persuade the world that it is less than it is. It need only continue its conversation with the moon and change moment to moment with the wind and light.

I know that you do not like your story. You see a sprawling series of missteps. Shallow explorations. Restless questing that led exactly nowhere. I see the slow work you have done to shift ancient continents below sea level. You are forgiven for not knowing what you didn't know and not seeing what you couldn't see.

What I see is that you are too big for containers, too luminous to be tucked away. You just want to be held—really held—in a way that will set you free. That's love's job. And the wildly brave act isn't to let it *in* as much as to let you *out*. Scatter yourself in the tree tops. Suffuse yourself across the twilit sky. Spread your phosphorescence over every soul you meet.

You are not too much. You are not.

Kate Godin writes and works in Western Massachusetts.

Conversation with a Whale
By Aubri Tallent

I walk through the ancient forest
until the ocean's edge,
hear the whale's spout and spray
drawing me closer.
I climb aboard smooth driftwood
setting myself to sea.

As my tears dissolve
into the salted depths beneath,
he rises to meet me,
magnificent eye envelops my gaze
and the words intoned in subsonic melody:

You were born
for this moment,
for this time,
on this ocean,
into this journey

to feel the fear that thumps and beats
just beneath the surface of your dreams
to know the aching of a child lost
to feel the skin as it's ripped from your bones
with the words:
your son has signs of severe brain injury,
to shed the skin of 11 years of marriage
to find only exposed blood and vital organs
sliding around underneath.

I know you are here
lying prostrate on driftwood,
untethered on this ocean,
certain you can't survive this,
repeating the only phrase left like a drum beat:
why, why, why?

Stop.
Breathe.
Now

feel the smooth solidity
of matter beneath you
cradling your weight.

Trust how every molecule
of salt and water
lifts you with its buoyancy.

Notice how the starlight reflection
spilling around us
knits ocean to sky.

And then listen,
hear my song
in alien deep
and human falsetto.

You are here
because you know the songs of the deep.

You are here to sing us home.

Aubri has been writing poetry since the age of five. Writing has become an incredible outlet in her life as she navigates the challenges of raising a child with cerebral palsy. She currently lives in Burlingame, CA and works as a life coach helping parents of kids with special needs reclaim their lives.

This Morning the Dam Broke
By Alison Oresman Wilson

To awaken as woman in full blossoming fire
Naked, prone, face up — nameless,
Splayed on a moss altar in Cathedral of Cedars at twilight
Moist as the morning dew.

Arching, aching for The Sun's unhurried, inexorable arrival
Longing to be pierced by the blinding light
As it touches and penetrates a powerful cresting wave
Before dissolving and receding into the infinity sea.

Do you have the audacity to name a wild wave?
Can you explain the droplets that create a majestic waterfall?
When and exactly what caused the dam to break?
Whatever shall we call the witness?

Language is the click of a camera shutter
Leaving a motionless picture behind.
Names stop the ever-breaking NOW dead,
A swinging tag on the toe of a corpse.

Another wave builds and breaks.
Hang 10 to love and joy.
Sing free-throated
And witness as the sound slowly dies and takes you with it.

Know this: There always is another rebirth.
Not yet named,
Unnamed and unknowable.

Love is perpetually blossoming.
Named or not,
Seen or unseen,
Heard or unheard.

Sink into your heart's cathedral,
Your true home.

Alison Oresman Wilson is a writer, light seeker, former hero-worshipper, and Founder of the Paradigm Shifters Super Heroes League and Creality Coaching. She believes that within each one of us is the hero we've been waiting for.

Garnet
By Lauren Oujiri

She expanded inside
The deep claret of space

Until she was outside it,
Burgundy, lustrous flows
Pulsing, beating red so red
Black blushed hot

She became a crimson ocean,
Erythrocyte chariots
Bounding the depths
With life's most
Precious treasure

Rising, falling, red,
Within-without, red

"Where am I?"

"Who am I?

"What am I?"

The strange fuschia words
Then floated down
A million rubicund rivulets
Converging to nothingness

She felt warmly alone
Under soft cardinal breast
Carmine stars twinkling
On her soles, in her fingertips,
Inside closed eyes,
Sinew, luminous epidermis

This Mars in her bones
Marrow of galaxy stillness
So ruby-rich
Auburn sanguine music in her
Hair, pomegranate scent
Pungent in her magenta fingertips

She gasped effervescent
beaujolais breaths
at every molecule,
Maroon beauty

Backward, forwards
Floating, as above so below,
Paradox fevered,
burning scarlet yet with
Softest pink grace
in this vast corpuscle

Wholly, holy red,
She became everything
Unalone, eternal She

Royal magnificence
Recognition of no-self,
The light, truth, love

The pure garnet heart

Lauren Oujiri, M.A., is a writer, coach, and reveler of life and love. She's an author and poet (haiku is her daily practice of gratitude and presence), and loves nothing more than listening to your stories, laughing, and dreaming deeply into the night. laurenoujiri.com; Instagram: @laurenoujiri

By Lauren Oujiri

La Planchadora
By Kimberly Blanchard

La Planchadora - Spanish word meaning ironing lady; in tango it refers to a woman who sits all night at a milonga without being asked to dance.

I waited in vain, and brushed the scarlet slashed skirt off my knee to reveal my twitching flesh. The last smudges of Chanel Rouge left my lips; like yesterday, the stained rim of my glass stole the last kiss. Your shadow swayed and stamped before me in a cloud of nostalgic happenstance.

I silently pleaded for your forgiveness, for one last chance. I betrayed you. I lied to you, claiming I adored you more than anyone. I abandoned you time and time again. I left you standing mid-dance, and went searching for something more. My heel tapped the blond wood one last time for your attention. I waited for your subtle cabeceo, for one final absolving twirl in the candlelight.

The vacuous space in my heart cried out into the echoing milonga in front of me. The twisting shadow, like the tear dropping into my empty goblet, was my own. The forsaken dancer this night, and every night, was my own lovelorn heart.

The mirror on the far wall, the elusive dancer, beckoned me. The melodic trance intensified as I slunk across the floor. I saw her. Her anguish ablaze with my rage. She had divorced me of dignity, as I had deceived her.

Standing before her, eyes cast at her rejected, beating heart, I asked for the way back. She led me to the vortex in the center, where pain, love, betrayal, and forgiveness intertwined in a fiery embrace. The violinist struck the final chord and let the bow fall to the ground. As did I.

Kimberly Blanchard is a writer, cross-cultural and executive coach, and a mother of two. She's a global nomad, having lived almost two decades out of the United States, where she recently repatriated to and calls New York City home.

The Substance of My Soul
By Guiomar Holme

For all that is beyond me, I come to you imploring
that what I say be heard:

That the weight of life be lifted,
for the substance of my soul
to open to the world, unfurl
the beauty of the rose.

To unveil from the smallest crack,
the light of the Divine,
and breathe from just that pin prick
the splendour of what's mine.

To bring what I've been seeking
into the world today —
the poetry that's needed
in order now to play.

To sleep in peace, wake rested,
to live a life with ease;
escape the prison of the mind,
from thought may I be freed.

Dissolve the knots of tension
from the shoulders of what is time;
Know that I will always be caught
by the net, forever mine.

If only, if only...

The magic of the heavens,
the spirits that surround,

the communion that is waiting,
are ready to be found.

Oh, for the tumult to subside,
for flowers eternal to spring;
for alignment with the rhythms —
poles united in a ring.

Oh, the substance of my soul,
to *feel* it and to *live!*
I reveal myself so fully;
it's all I have to give.

The heaviness is lifted.
Smiling,
From the depths of my existence.

We Decided to Exist
By Meagan Adele Lopez

Together, you and I, we started our lives,

Practicing with Barbie how to be good wives.

Sometimes our Barbie had quite a sick mind,

So, we slapped her wrist to put her in line.

Then came Nintendo. Mario had business,

It was *his* job to save Peach Princess.

She is helpless, we learned, without a man.

So, we listened to Peach; we were big fans.

As men came and went, including our fathers,

We wondered what would make us good daughters.

We asked, "Is it TV that shows us the way?"

The women become moms; dads work; kids play.

Okay.

Look pretty, smile big, pad those tiny breasts.

Lose weight, drink wine, smoke cigarettes!

One plus one equals unworthy of love;

We'll let some things slide, including a shove.

Because Ken is just Ken: "give him some slack!"

The whole wide world weighs on his poor back.

All *we* have to do is have his babies,

Or else, shrivel up and become cat ladies.

Tis the worst-ist fate you ever could see

To be a maiden alone without a 'he.'

Just lay down submissive (they paint the picture),

It isn't worth fighting; it's in the scripture.

We don't have a say in where our lives go

It was pre-written in our embryos.

Our bodies were just meant to procreate.

Being a mother can *only* be great.

We don't have a choice; what's assumed is true:

Our sole role is to choose: pink sheets or blue?

We look at our girlfriends, who fall in line fast

We gulp our wine back from the tall glass.

We look at our men shining so bright.

Would they *like* us if we put up a fight?

Could *you* choose *you* and still have a right

To be loved by a man in your own light?

Without kids or attachments of marriage

Driving yourself in your own red carriage,

Just freedom, train rides and fires for two

No more, nothing less—just you and your boo.

Forget it. Too hard. Just go with the flow.

Paddling upstream packs too hard of a blow.

It's easier this way...

Don't stray.

Easier...until the voices come out,

The soft voices that we all like to doubt,

"My darling friend, you no longer have to hide.

We've gone through it and come out the other side."

Shut up!

We muffle them, stomp on them, put them to rest.

The knots pile up in our backs and our chests.

"Despite what you think, *your* dreams matter most.

If you ignore them your soul will ghost.

If you listen, freedom and love *will* lead,

All the pain that you've built up *will* recede.

I won't deny you may be put through tests,

Stay true, stay strong, you deserve what is next.

When you choose your soul, your unique riverbed

The rest will follow, and you will be led.

Don't you see?"

We smiled to each other,

To Barbie and to Princess.

We didn't slap their wrists.

Or ours.

We decided to just exist.

Meagan Adele Lopez wrote her first novel, <u>Three Questions: Because a Quarter Life Needs Answers</u>, after she quit Hollywood as an actress. Her second novel, <u>The Academy</u>, is coming soon. She currently lives in Paris.

The Truth
By Joy Brill

I have not abandoned the plan for my life that I created with God
The miraculous residue of my birth will not be washed away
I am the designer of my dreams
The architect of my truth

A brave woman who met the abyss with terror and challenged it.

Bliss
By Joy Brill

the gift of no
by Cristine Reynaert

when children are placed
in wide-open space
they keep to the center
unsure just how far
to explore

but watch them run free
once boundaries are set
released from the fear
of losing themselves
as they play

it's the same with your heart

to know she's safe
to explore her space
spread out her love
and do the work
she's meant to do

to say the yesses
she's meant to say

your heart needs you
to say no

Cristine Reynaert can't quite put her gratitude for words into words.
But she joyfully shares more of them at <u>www.instagram.com/ccrpoetry/</u>.

Into the World
By Rachel Bruns

I step into a vast, wide space
Sun waning, splintered light,
In search of something, maybe nothing
Waiting in between
Two truths that pull and push and fray, refusing to resolve,
Refusing to concede the point; they know they each belong.

I walked into the world on time, determined to belong.
To grasp and feel and claim my space
And live with fierce resolve.
I searched and hunted for the thing; I thought it was the light.
I landed, lingered somewhere else, on thresholds in between –
Surprised to be content with nothing

In everything and nothing
I'm a speck that must belong
To the time I'm here beyond, between —
Saluting all this space.
I usher in the grandness, taking in the light.
There's nothing here to solve.

Pulling at the tangled hurt — why won't it just resolve?
Wanting nothing
More than light
And to know that I belong.
So we find a way together and wander through the space
To make the most of time between.

The sound, it flies between
These bookends, never to resolve.
It echoes through a space
Of nothing.
Only there it does belong.
And so do we — to the light.

The question finds delight
With no answer in between.
It knows it still belongs.
Its only promise to resolve
Nothing.
Only making me the answer, as I sit here small in space.

In this light of stillness, I choose never to resolve.
Instead, I claim the in-between and what I came here for: nothing.
Where everything belongs. This hushed and holy space.

Rachel is a coach, advocate, and writer who spends her days pondering the mysteries of the universe, plotting a takedown of the white-supremacist, capitalist patriarchy, and enjoying the company of trees, clouds, and flowers. You can connect with her at rachelbrunscoaching.com.

How Silvermoon Found Her Heart, Her Purpose and a Friend
By Leigh Ann Kittell

With a swoosh of her tail, Silvermoon swam away from the teachers. Her sensitive heart hung heavy from their criticism of her swimming skills and she tried to look strong. She searched for her friends, but they had left. The young merman she secretly admired spoke with another girl.

She thought, "I will show them I can swim!"

When she set out into the ocean, a strong current whisked Silvermoon away, down a chute, to the depths of the ocean.

Her teachers knew. The curse. They scurried to gather the elders.

When Silvermoon hit the bottom of the sea, her silvery scales reflected a lunar light. Looking up, her eyes met the glow of the Pearl. Silvermoon had heard the elders speak of its dangers, but she could not resist its attraction.

Silvermoon sensed her longings, desires, and fantasies fulfilled as she moved towards the Pearl. Her lost parents held her. The merman kissed her. Friends admired her. Teachers praised her.

The elders at the coral reef shook their heads with grief. No mermaid had ever returned from the enchantment of the Pearl.

Rana, a queen sting ray, circled around the group and spoke, "I can swim to the bottom of the cave, but only Silvermoon can break the Curse. See her strong and free, and she will save you from future danger."

The superstitious mermaids feared Rana's powers and reluctantly agreed to her plan. The young ones who overheard Rana gathered in vigil for Silvermoon, sending her good thoughts of strength and freedom.

By the time Rana reached the bottom of the sea, the Pearl had spun threads around Silvermoon. Rana spoke to her and said, "You may stay, Silvermoon. But I would like to have your heart and return it home?"

Her inner voice said, "No, I want to keep my heart."

When Silvermoon defended her heart, the Pearl's threads began to break. The Pearl fought back by enticing her with more delusions of love.

Coming closer, Rana demanded her heart more forcefully.

Silvermoon freed her hands from the Pearl to protect it.

Losing its grip on Silvermoon, the Pearl spun another web around her.

With grace and speed, Rana slipped her thin yet lethal body in front of Silvermoon and moved towards her heart.

Silvermoon shouted, "No, I will not give you my heart. It is mine!"

By the time she spoke, Rana had darted away and Silvermoon was shouting directly at the Pearl.

The Pearl's power vanished.

Awoken from her trance, Silvermoon clutched her heart. Rana held her tight in her wings to support her.

She looked at Rana and said: "My heart. My heart. It is mine. Not my parents', not my partner's, not my elders' or my friends'. Mine."

The Pearl dissolved never to enchant again.

Silvermoon's body swelled with strength. With Rana at her side, she navigated the waters home.

Her friends rejoiced.

The elders bowed in gratitude.

Silvermoon found her heart, her purpose, and a friend.

Leigh Ann Kittell is a certified Martha Beck Life Coach, yoga teacher, and writer with an unquenchable curiosity about how to transcend the challenges of everyday life through self-help, self-development, and modern spiritual practices. Her first book, The Easy Way to Enlightenment — How to Show Your Soul the Adventure of Your Life, will be published in 2018. www.leighannkittell.com

I Finally Tell My Truth
By Cindy Lou Levee/ Natanya

On the first day of a seminar ten miles from Alcatraz, we Leaping Poets did what we do best:

We Leapt.

A student across the table with a huge Afro reminded me of the prominent countercultural activist Angela Davis. But she said, "I'm Mona Lisa Saloy from New Orleans, and I write about my African-American community."

Somebody else from the Big Easy way out here on my first day at San Francisco State University?! I'd never been in class with a Black student because I grew up during the era of segregation.

I was so excited I almost fell off my chair, like I used to as a child when I laughed too hard and too loud at the dinner table and Mama got mad because girls and women were supposed to act like ladies—except for Mardi Gras costume parties. Once I rubbed black beeswax greasepaint around my eyes and became a football player for my neighbor's "Dress As Your Secret Desire."

Finally it was my turn at our poetry table, "I'm Cindy Levy from New Orleans, and I write about my Jewish community."

I darted straight to this Mona Lisa as soon as our poetry teacher called it quits. Even though I was born into a Jewish family, I'd eaten African American soul food—fried chicken, collard greens, breaded fried okra, cornbread, and hushpuppies—all my life as a Southerner. Powerful Black women had helped raise me in the racist 1950s and 60s when such women could only get work as helpers for white families.

Mission blue butterflies flitted by as we two poets rambled around our fog-shrouded campus, talking and talking. When we traded poems, she said, "You're a sincere white girl."

I hadn't even realized what was missing, but I felt more balanced with Mona Lisa. I yearned for more. With our country in ferment socially, culturally, politically, religiously, and spiritually in the 1970s, we were part of a new humanity that I hadn't known existed.

She was born when her namesake, the *Mona Lisa*, toured the United States, and she soon toured, taught, gave readings and eventually sold her books, winning the T.S. Eliot Prize for Poetry.

Some people get to express themselves and tell their truth from the time they're born, but many of us don't. That included me. But after landing out West amongst the chaparral, rabbits, hawks, redwoods, sea lions and deer, I didn't have to remain silent anymore, either. I found out that the United Nations' International Bill of Human Rights, signed just after World War II by all the major nations on Earth, proclaimed that individuals can express what they believe without fear. I hoped that would become a reality.

Cindy changed her last name from L-E-V-Y to L-E-V-E-E in honor of the embankments built to hold back the waters of the Mississippi and Lake Ponchartrain from the land she grew up on. Spring floods deposit silt along the rivers, creating natural levees, the high land along the waterways. Levees support the growth of hardwood forests and provide land dry enough for cultivation and habitation.

Lucky Fish
By Melissa Pennel

Yes, the teacher liked my writing. But maybe I won blue ribbons because I was just the only kid who ever had a chance?

Perhaps Willie could've written better if his parents weren't cousins, or Charlotte could've won blue ribbons if her dad didn't shoot heroin every night.

Through the years, my fantastical blue ribbon stories became dramatic adolescent outbursts. "Every other girl has kissed a boy!" filled pages once reserved for the meanderings of my imagination; I stopped chasing fairies with my pen, and instead worried why boys weren't chasing me.

"Give the people what they want!" was the accidental mantra, the one I never said out loud.

The people didn't want creativity and originality, I decided; they wanted you to look like them, to smile, to starve yourself, if that's what it takes!

Oh, and could you make it all look effortless, too?

It was unconscious, this slow unraveling of my individuality, but before long "What do you like to do?" became a question I looked to my left and right for. "Yes, what *she* likes, what *you* like, that's what I like too!"

It's no wonder that when I tried to dive back into my well of imagination, one that once held fairies and shapeshifters and ghosts, I found only tumble-weeds. "I'm just not creative" became the new mantra, the one I never said out loud.

Blank pages, furrowed brow, confusion over where it all had gone. Was I ever a writer, a creator? Maybe I'd just been a lucky fish in a disadvantaged pond?

"When you peel the onion of self, it might make you cry," I read one day in a magazine. I was an adult now, functioning just fine, thank-you-very-much, but this phrase made me put down my coffee cup.

Do I have an onion of self?

I imagined myself layered with years of self-criticism and interests borrowed from others. I looked at my coffee cup, the one I filled with a pound of sugar just to choke down.

Do I even like coffee?

The internal Spanish Inquisition began: Do I actually like running, or do I just think I should? Do I really like wine tasting, or punk shows, or flea markets? The layers looked so much like me that I wasn't even sure there was an onion to peel. But slowly the blank pages began to fill up, the frustrated "I'm just not creative" replaced with "maybe I like this" or "I know I used to like that." Stories started coming out in gasping spurts, like pulling teeth but still…writing.

It took a long time to put on these layers of my onion, and it's taking a long time to peel them away. But I know that deep down, somewhere, is a girl who used to write with reckless abandon and create without considering what was "good" or "acceptable." A girl who lived by a true mantra, one she *could* say out loud: "Don't worry about what the other fish in the pond are doing."

I know she's in there, I've just got to keep peeling the layers back.

Melissa Pennel is a writer and an overthinker from Sacramento, California. She enjoys vegan fast food, jumping on trampolines, and being way more obsessed with her cats than she likes to let on publicly. You can find more of her writing on followyourfirecoaching.com.

The Path to Our True Selves: A Letter for the Journey
By Hyeon-Ju Rho

At 42, reeling from a new baby and professional turmoil, I realized that I didn't need a new job or other external change. I needed to find my way to a truer version of myself. This was no easy feat for someone whose sense of self depended on masterfully being what others expected me to be. The enterprise of becoming myself felt very much like walking into an abyss. This is the letter I wish I'd had then, and a love letter for anyone embarking on this journey now.

Dear Traveler,

Pain brought you here. This is as it should be. The path becomes visible when you're broken apart. When your masks were still in place, your vision was too hemmed-in to see this place.

Ahead of you are the questions you've kept at bay your whole life. What's here when the masks are stripped away? Is there anything worth loving?

Know that this is a journey of courage, and that in standing here, you are brave. You may hear voices, internal and external, telling you that your undertaking is selfish, foolish, self-indulgent, maybe even pathetic. It will hurt, but come back in these moments to the pain of what you've lived through already. The loneliness, despair and dark hopelessness — all of that was, is, real. And the only way out is through.

At first, the uncertainty of it all will unnerve you. You'll want the answers, and to have them now. Remember that you've spent decades looking away from yourself. To shift now, to hear a voice that's been silent, to learn a language never before spoken—these are unfamiliar practices. Give yourself the same patience and gentleness you would give a child taking her first steps.

The initial signs will be small—a color you're drawn to, a quote you can't get out of your head, something you see that sparks a feeling of life. Go toward these things and keep them close, regardless of whether they make any logical sense. The connection you feel is nourishment. The more you feed your true self, the hungrier she will be and the more specific her demands. Keep feeding her.

Some of the discoveries will require you to go against what others expect of you. This will be uncomfortable, but it's a sign you're making progress. Take stock here of how far you've come, how much you've risked already, and how close you might be to tasting something resembling wholeness. Be ruthless.

Beacon of Light
Sheringham Point Lighthouse
Shirley, Vancouver Island, British Columbia, Canada
By Ingrid Bizio

Keep going.

Keep your eyes and heart open for the gifts that will come to you. The chance encounter with someone who does the work you would love to do if it weren't so impractical, the call offering the thing you've been afraid to admit you want.

It will be easy to feel cynical and dismissive of these coincidences. Be skeptical if you must, but accept the gifts. Doors will open. Just walk through.

Somewhere along the way you'll notice that you're no longer alone. You will sense the presence of someone who feels both familiar and new. The pleasure you feel in her company will be something beyond questions of acceptability or presentability. There has never been anyone like her, and as you allow yourself to see her uniqueness, her beauty will move you. Embrace her. Let yourself love her. This is who you have always been.

Look around you now. Notice that the path is holding you, has been holding you all along. Come and feel the sunlight on your own skin, the joy of taking up your own precious space in this wild and beautiful world. Walk, dance, it doesn't matter. Your life is waiting.

With love and affection,
The Universe

I am a wife, mother and professional coach. I am also the old woman at the edge of the woods, the wild girl who dances as she walks, and the monastic who finds life in a moment of quiet. You can find more of my writing at www.hjrho.com.

II.
BECOMING

At Peace with the Pace of Transformation
By Katrina Allen
katrinaallenart.com

OVERCOMING

Mammal That You Are
By Julie Finelli

Mammal that you are, you will come up for air. Sacred design assures you are not asked to hold your breath forever. Your creator does not expect you to endure an eternal watery abyss. Right now, yes, you are going down, to the dark underwater. Yet know you will return and breathe at the surface once again. Under. Up. A thousand times over, and then a thousand times more.

Gasping and gulping for air you will rise each time from the underneath, and things will look new when you catch your breath. Every time you break through the surface, you will sense yourself and your view with soggy, softer, blurrier edges that hardly pass for boundaries. With every ascent, repulsion drowning in fear faithfully gives way to swelling flows of merciful curiosity.

This cycle is glorious, and it is horrific. Know your store of resilience is not only enough, it is stunningly expansive. The vastness of your courage overflows what you think ordinary can survive to hold. Yes, you will cry. You will ache. My God, you will tremble. But there will also be laughter. Awe. Love. You are privy to the depths, and thus the heights. Lucky you.

Up from the bottom you detect your movement toward peace, as the gray mixed from dark and light becomes brilliantly hued. You experience the tints and tones of forms, of minds, of spirits, as you never did before your time inside the sea. You soak in nuances and sense them from all sides, perceive them from the inside out, with gallons more acuity than the untried soul can.

You have grown familiar with truth's pattern, how it crashes over you in waves, knocking you under, and then reaches back out to keep you afloat. Now you know you are brave. In moments, you are less afraid. In flashes, you are unafraid. Today's oceans of sorrow below skies of fear may even transform to creeks in the clouds.

You will absorb your life at the water. You will swirl your ins and outs of the sea to make hope. You will carry this hope with you like an oxygen tank, for if ever again, whenever again, you plummet before you rise.

Julie Finelli danced on Broadway, performed stand-up, wrote bestsellers, and now hosts a wildly clever podcast, all in her fantasy life. When not busy with what exists only in her head, she reads, works to break the code of raising children into solid citizens, and wishes she would get more done.

Very Superstitious
By Tonya Collings Crombie

I know what you're thinking. You think that it's there waiting to happen. You're looking backwards and making note of the terrible things that haven't happened. Not to you, not to your parents, or even to your grandparents. Somehow you think that means that it has to happen soon — like the sword of Damocles, or the San Andreas fault, just tick tick ticking... waiting. Bad things have to happen eventually, you think. If it hasn't happened yet, it's just a matter of time.

But that isn't how it works. I never promised it would be easy, but I didn't promise to keep score, either. There isn't a divine algorithm or a time-table. There will be pain, but also exquisite joy. If you do it right, the joy will always outweigh the pain. It's how I designed you.

Your superstitions aren't true. They aren't real. But I need to tell you something that is true: when you're deep, deep in the pain, it won't feel that way. It won't feel as if the joy could possibly outweigh the heavy misery you will find your-self in. You may not be able to see past that moment. I want you to hear me and repeat this as you wiggle your toes and breathe another breath, like Dorothy tapping her ruby slippers, "This too shall pass. This too shall pass. This too shall pass."

It will.

I promise you.

It always does.

Always.

You don't have to get through another day, or another hour... just another breath. And you will. You just did.

And the joy will return when you aren't even looking for it. It'll sneak in like the first cold day after an unbearably hot summer, and you'll quickly forget how hot you were, or how sad, or lost, or ashamed.

This I promise you, my sweet, sweet girl with the very big heart. Big hearts feel big pain, but they also feel big joy. You will always come back to big joy. When you doubt it, when the night is dark and fear and grief are all you can see, remember:

Wiggle your toes.

Breathe your breath.

This too shall pass.

Tonya Crombie is a wife, mother of two teenagers and two dogs, a coach, and a lover of things ridiculous and irreverent. She spends her time trying to figure out who she wants to be when she grows up and reminding herself to notice the amazing beauty that surrounds her each day.

Reconciliation
By Rhonda Jean Seiter

You are not the Amazonian child lying in the belly of the anaconda,
nor Kitty Genovese dead on her apartment stoop,
although your present situation lends such a perspective.

You curl in fetal position in the depths of the pit,
and do not see the walls of the womb.
What does a fetus know of earth as it gestates toward birth?
What do we know of eternity
while brushing our molars and bandaging our tattered soles?
These well-like walls surround you
because you have mistaken your house for your home.
You seek truth among the nine-to-five —
your fall was inevitable.

You gaze into the eyes of your most beloved,
and see they cannot help you.
The uninitiated yell down through cupped hands —
It's all good.
Breathe and count to ten.
Visualize a beach.
Help is on the way.
What do they know of hell?
Their sweat is free from blood and debris.
You resent their expressionless faces.
This anger will fuel your momentum.
You acknowledge you are alone,
which is the beginning of the way out, your quickening.

Your eyes adjust, yet your hands are not visible.
Scratch your palms.
Scratch the soles of your feet.
You are alive!
Feel the swell of your chest.
Place your hand on your heart.
Constricting in fear and panic will get you nowhere.
Unfurl into this sunless spring.
Follow the tiniest impulse.

Be still even as you run.
Quiet your mindless brain as it tirelessly works toward a solution.
A logical answer is not your exit strategy.
Be as silent and alert as the grazing gazelle after the lioness arrives.
Curiosity is your companion.

Trust the way out will reveal itself
even as you rage that God has abandoned you.
"Now hear this, O foolish and senseless people,
who have eyes but do not see; who have ears but do not hear."
Even the best from the golden-edged pages cannot be read in the dark.
The universe will offer its wisdom flowing through and around you
in the infinite suns and black holes of your being.

Do not dwell on death, although the pain is unbearable.
Find the place that doesn't throb—be grateful for it.
Recall the most precious pleasures,
and stitch these images to your sorrows.
Are we decaying toward dying or unfolding into living?
We are movement either way.
Inhale will follow exhale with no effort on your part.
You are alive!
Hurl a prayer of gratitude along with the expletives.
Do not deny yourself this pleasure.

Be awestruck when you discover that the doula
holding your newborn a decade after your mother's death
coincidentally bought your childhood home.
Heed flitting imagery that shines brightly in your mind's eye
while your rods and cones lie dormant.
This uncommon communication will guide you toward the light.

Heaven is not freedom from hell.
It is a reconciliation beyond duality,
a weaving together of a new creation until your frazzled nerves
settle calmly into the deeper knowing.

Rhonda Jean Seiter lives in California. During her summers as a high school teacher,
she traveled through every continent except Antarctica. The wonder of gazing into
her newborn's eyes has been unsurpassed. She is currently writing a memoir about
her unconventional journey to motherhood. (Rjseiter@aol.com)

Limitless Mind
By Rhonda Jean Seiter
Mixed media on canvas
10 x 12 inches

Traveling Notes for This Abyss
By Shana Brodnax

You are about to climb down into the well—the seemingly depthless well of pain that you have been glossing over, pushing down, locking away, or rushing past your entire life. I'll start with the harshest truth, so you'll know that you can trust the rest of what I say:

Every iota of that pain is down there. You will be spared nothing.

For the time that you travel through this dark night of the soul, you will live within a shroud. You will slog through every step. You'll wonder more than once if you will survive. I'll tell you now the bittersweet answer: you will. You will face it all, and you will heal it all, and you will emerge on the other side in one whole beautiful piece.

As a fellow traveler of this abyss, with the fresh memory of its shadows, and with all the love in my broken open heart—here is what I offer you:

• Nothing you do can make the journey shorter or safer or less painful. Give up any attempt to control it or to enforce a timeline. The process is whole within itself, and unknowable, and it will lead you—trust it and surrender to it. Also, healing is not erasure: you're not going to reach a place where you're past your grief. There will be scars, and they will mark you as a warrior.

• Nothing will help, and everything will help. Read everything. Try all the programs. Talk with your therapist. Take online courses. Do your work. Follow every single nudge from your intuition. Write. Pray. Meditate. Forgive. Walk. Run. Go to yoga. Cry out to the ocean. Your sorrow will be waiting for you everywhere, and it will all seem pointless, but it's not. You're surviving another day, and you're gathering tools for how to live as the person you'll be when you climb back out.

• You are loved. Reach out. Allow your kindred to witness your suffering—they will be honored to hold space for you. Ask for help. Ask for exactly what you need. Ask every day. Ask God. Ask the universe. Ask all your totems and angels and intermediaries. Ask your ancestors and your future self. You have to go by yourself, but you're not in this alone.

• Don't resist the pain. Breathe deeply and soften into it. If you allow it to flow, it will eventually flow out of you—it just wants to be felt. It won't take you down or take you over. It will teach you. Let it be and let it go.

• Show yourself complete and relentless compassion. Take exquisitely good care of yourself. Listen to your body and spirit. Set the boundaries you need and stand by them as if you're fighting for your life—because you are.

This is your becoming.

Shana Brodnax is a life and leadership coach who supports people in bringing their best and whole selves to the things that matter to them—using wisdom from and strategies for the mind, body, heart, and spirit. More information about her approach can be found at www.3birdscoaching.com.

To You, the Person Heading Into the Abyss
By Ingrid Bizio

You look so scared right now, just like I did, all those years ago. I wish I could spare you all the things that are about to happen to you. I wish I could tell you that this isn't going to hurt—a lot! I can't tell you any of that, but I can tell you that you *will* survive this and that you *will* endure and come out the other side stronger, wiser and happier. Know that this storm *will* pass, that it won't rain forever and that the sun will shine again, even for you!

Most of all I want to tell you that this is not your fault.

I wish I hadn't been so afraid. I wish I had always remembered my own truth and my own strength. There were days when I was sure I would never see daylight again. I doubted myself every day, but eventually I just listened to my inner voice and my intuition. I found that guiding light inside me again. I knew it was there! It had always been there, I had just forgotten about it and the voices in my head tried very hard to push me away from it at times. Finally I turned them off and listened to my own heart and only that. I knew it would never steer me wrong. I kept believing what I had known about myself all along: that I am strong, that I am lovable and that I am worth all the effort this took.

I learned that I could do all the things that were asked of me because I am so much more powerful than I gave myself credit for. I had to remind myself from time to time that I was so deserving of the peace I would gain once this was all over and that I had so much love to give. I did not let myself be deterred by obstacles along the way. I never gave up, even when it seemed like that would be the easiest way out.

And now I promise you these things: you will come out of this alive; there is light outside of this cave; you will get to know yourself again; you will rediscover all those qualities about yourself that you had long forgotten and— you will be better for all of it!

Ingrid has had an interest in books and foreign languages since childhood in Germany. She immigrated to Canada at age 23, has three grown children and one granddaughter. Ingrid has done inspirational writing on her Facebook page. She currently resides in Medicine Hat, Alberta, Canada.

Postcard From the Ledge
By Allyson Linehan

My dear friend,

Look up at the sky before you descend into the cave. Savor every color, take in every cloud. On the dark and dreary days that follow, you will need to hold within you every beam of light.

When you first hit the wall of total darkness, you may want to hold your breath and run as fast and as far as possible, but try not to. Sit in the stillness, breathe, and get to know this place, for it will be your home for quite some time.

The hardest part is feeling you are by yourself, sloshing through the mud, eating cobwebs for breakfast. Sometimes you might see others on a similar journey; you will recognize them by the desperation in their eyes. Lend them any comfort you can spare, as you will need theirs later.

Look for clues as you go—dreams that point in new directions, books that fall to your feet, words yelled down and echoing through the boulders—anything that gives you a moment's pause in the darkness. They may be small but each step takes you to your next right step, and that is probably all you can handle right now.

Take care of yourself as best you can. Bathe yourself in the subterranean pools and anoint the fissures of your skin with fragrant oils, caress your sores and scabs with gentle hands, as they have been through so much. Hold an orange reverently, engaging all of your senses, as you let it feed your soul. Live in the crunch of celery. And when you stop and quench your thirst, taste all the glaciers it has passed through and let it cool longings you have never dared to speak.

The cave takes in all it hears—the shouted curses, deepest cries and most joyous hallelujahs—and turns them into prayers for you.

And when you are so tired you can't move, let your inner child take a nap. Rest, dreams and the breeze through your window will restore you enough to face another day. Then do it again and again. I will hold you in a sacred space until your re-emergence.

All I ask is that when you are leaving this cave, bruised, battered but more alive and awake, take the time to let the next one know, they, too, will make it out alive.

I am Allyson Linehan, mother of two sons, who have shown me how to show up in all of our lives, that they didn't need the perfect life I thought they wanted, they needed flesh and blood me. We are emerging back into the light, savoring our growth and connections.

LIFEJacket
By Tracy Weber, Ph.D.

Miles of cool lake glisten in the sunlight as clouds create shadows on the mirrored surface. I feel proud of the simple accomplishment in rising early to kayak. While sensing unbalance in the plastic boat, I drink in the beauty around me, reflecting on my blessings to be here, in this moment, healthy, strong, enjoying serenity.

Treasure Island in the distance will be my destination. Dig into the water; first left, then right. Dig deeper to go faster to reach the goal sooner; coasting lets momentum carry me forward. Slow progress suspends time and I question the goal. I consider turning back. I weigh my options, there's nothing imminent waiting for me and no physical pain to use as an excuse. Shifting to get more comfortable on the hard seat, I straighten my legs and wiggle my toes inside my damp water shoes.

The illusion of the island appearing close reminds me of when I climbed Sleeping Bear Dunes; Lake Michigan teasingly just over the next sand hill. I remember not persevering to the shore's edge; this time I double-down on my resolve to reach my destination.

My body paddles while my mind relaxes, creating metaphors about mysteries hiding beneath me in the deep, dark water. I notice the weight of my necklace between my breasts. It's a metal medallion, the centaur logo Paul created. A wave of sadness comes over me as I relive his recent death.

Finally, shallow waters begin to display a bed of vibrantly colored rocks. I hear the bottom of the boat scrape when they abruptly slow my forward movement. I take a deep breath, relishing in my successful arrival at the island's edge. My brief moment of triumph quickly turns to the realization that I must repeat the long trip. Sigh.

No other choice, I get to work. Paddle. Paddle. I head towards the tower, the landmark for our cottage on the densely populated lakeshore. Winds kick up, fear creeps in. I regret not having practiced tipping the kayak over and climbing back in. I remind myself I am a strong swimmer.

Halfway across the lake, I realize I'm heading toward the wrong tower, adding a long stretch of lakeshore to my journey. Disappointed by my miscalculation, I recognize that once again the only choice is to continue paddling.

Finally, I am passing cottages I recognize; fatigue is replaced by a sense of accomplishment. I'm greeted by my husband, who questions why I was gone so long. I share my story with pride. We laugh about my "directional challenges" that occur on land, as well as on water. Helping me carry the kayak up the hill, he notices there isn't a life jacket in it. He angrily scolds me; his fear for what could have gone terribly wrong presenting itself as loud, hostile disappointment.

No life jacket could be a story-changer if I let it. I choose to reflect on my blessings to be here, in this moment, healthy, strong, and safely home.

Tracy Weber, Ph.D., is an equine-assisted learning (EAL) facilitator, founder of Kaleidoscope (www.myklc.com), and author of Wildly Successful (www.wildlysuccessfulsolutions.com). She partners experientially with four-legged facilitators to co-create life-changing and transformational experiences. Tracy's TEDxSVSU, "Horse Wisdom for the Human World," is a fun and entertaining way to learn about EAL.

The Light Through the Window
By Keri Clarke

I know you're scared. Their dynamic has terrified you since you were a young girl, in your darkened room, covers pulled over your head, echoes of their shouting voices curling around your heart like icy fingers. It was not your fault then, and it is not your responsibility now.

You have been led gently in your own journey of healing so you will see, finally, that although you are their daughter, they are the ones frozen in a childish dance. Their desperation calls you not to fix things, but rather to lead them to the light. You do not do this by telling, but rather by continuing on your journey of healing and joy. They are stuck in this way of being like soldiers in a bunker, with fighting all around. They know the only way to freedom is to open the door and risk vulnerability, but they're so afraid of more pain that they stay, complaining in their lonely prisons.

By living in truth, you begin to chisel a space for a window so they can see the light pouring in, and that they are actually safe. Have courage, and know that you will continue to receive gifts in this journey, and when the time comes, you will be ready.

Trust yourself to tell the truth despite the courage it requires. You were always meant to lead. Square your shoulders and build the window so they can see the light.

Keri's professions have included Equine Science, Balloon-Animal Tying, Design, Branding, Business, Copywriting and Podcasting (although not in that order). She loves the smell of woodsmoke in winter and the sound of hoofbeats on pine needles. She is now training to be a life coach and author.

The Agony, The Shift, The Blessing
By Lois Melkonian

Once upon a time you played the piano tirelessly, mastered Johannes Sebastian Bach's "Invention Number 1," but on stage you collapsed in fear.

And you were humiliated.

Once upon a time you were noticed for the first time as a beautiful woman and were seduced, enjoying every minute of the attention until you realized you didn't want *that*.

And you were raped.

Once upon a time you worked 12 hours a day to get the story right, delivered it to your audience and won awards for your compelling achievements.

And you got replaced.

Once upon a time you took care of your mother who was dying at home and stayed with her through thick and thin and was her defender and protector.

And she died.

Life sucks sometimes.

Then the darkness hovered and swallowed up the light. You sat on the chaise lounge where your mother's last days were spent and re-lived your losses. The stories took shape and flashed in muted colors. You were surrounded by sounds and smells. The pain was deep but you remained, attached to your stories. The memories continued until there was nothing more to remember. There were no more tears. And that's when you understood. The stories were over.

In that early morning, the darkness released its hold as sunlight poured through the window. Slowly, slowly it began to illuminate: your face, your hands, your chest, your legs until your whole body was radiant. The prisms of light found their way inside, casting a spectrum of color on every dark crevice, redeeming your nightmares one by one.

Your son plays the piano more beautifully than you could ever imagine.
You're with your soul mate who loves you unconditionally.
You're writing and working on projects you're passionate about.
Your mother is free and so are you.

Life still sucks sometimes.

Yet you discovered that being scorned, beaten down, passed over and crushed actually made you stronger.

So I leave you now with these beatitudes, your blessed supremeness.

Blessed are those who are shunned, for they will see their children thrive.
Blessed are those who are violated, for they shall receive love beyond compare.
Blessed are those who are falsely accused, for they shall live an abundant life.
Blessed are those who mourn, for they shall be comforted.

A gritty, intense believer, Lois has been telling stories all her life. When she stumbled into "Write into Light," she reconnected with a hidden longing to share truth without holding back. Her goal? To find redemption in every story. And maybe some strong coffee and dark chocolate.

Darkness and Light
By Lois Melkonian

The Journey
By LK Toepfer

Ah, my friend.

You are heading into the abyss.

I yell for you to stop—turn back, run the other way.
Find some sunshine; smell the flowers and ignore this cruel world.
But my voice is carried off by the wind. You no longer hear me.
You are destined to move forward into the unknown.

I watch as you enter alone, and all I can do is pray.
I watch you step into the shadows and become swallowed whole.
It is as if the universe has conspired to leave you with no other options.
You are headed for heartbreak, and I am powerless to save you.

With all my heart, I wish I could give you light through this darkness.
With all my heart, I wish I could prevent the pain you will receive.
With all my heart, I wish I could wrap my arms around you and protect your soul.
But I cannot. You will be challenged, and I will be unable to block the scars.

So, I pray you know this: It will not be fatal.

I pray you find a way to fight back and push through.
I pray you dig deep within your core and find the strength you doubted you possessed.
I pray you realize that you are guided by an inner wisdom.
I pray you hear your soul softly say: "You've got this. Don't give up yet."

I pray that you trust you will live.

I imagine you are somewhere deep within the void, and you find a rock.
A simple, smooth rock that looks like a good place to sit.
I imagine you stumbling upon it, sinking onto its cool surface, and catching your breath.
I smile and imagine you are grateful for the rest.

As you sit, you pause and breathe in the quiet around you.
After a moment, you notice a faint glow in the distance.
It is soft, and feels inviting to you.
I sense your heart leaning towards this comforting light.

You decide to get up and walk towards this comfort.
As you move closer to the light, you realize you are leaving the abyss.
You stumble upon sunlight, and stand for a moment, enjoying its warmth.
My heart fills with joy as I sense you absorb the vast beauty surrounding you.

I say prayers of thanks that you have finally passed through the darkness.
I watch you release the burdens that your body and soul have been carrying.
My heart warms as you shed the skin that carries the wounds of your past.
And I add my prayers of gratitude to the winds that whisper across your soul,
speaking the words you have been searching for:

Welcome home.

Writer, Dreamer, and Explorer. Some days, the coffee kicks in and I slay the dragon. Other days, I hide under the covers. Every day, I am grateful for this messy mud bath we call life. May we all touch our dreams. Namaste.

Forward
By Francine Yacintha

To the little girl in the cloak of womanhood
To hear the call and pull towards your truth
Is never an easy task,
And we know how clueless you were.

"You were once one
Scattered into infinity
Pieces with voices to sing
The stories of freedom and love"

Slowly the walls of invisible prisons dissolved.
One by one you managed to set them free.
Now, it is never about the reward set on the journey,
But simply following the heart's yearning

Knowing that deep in your bones,
You sit in an empty space
And find yourself whole,
As a new untamed path opens up
To the freedom that is graced as your birthright.

You will receive guidance, protection, and companionship
Because you will never be alone
Even when loneliness is lurking behind the heart.

Be bitter if you must,
But not too bitter so your heart
Can melt into the sweetness that is you.

Be joyous if you must,
But not too joyous so your heart
Can enter into the stillness that is you.

Be grateful if you must,
For gratefulness is your nature
Sitting in harmony with the wonders of Life.

"If the sun rises after the night comes to an end,
Can joy return after we suffered pain?

If the trees grow back after the winter's end,
Can love return after we were broken open?"

Let's move forward, my dear friend,
You are ready.

Another student of life who loves to travel

Canyon Gift Shop Now Open
By Kate DeSmet

To the middle-aged woman hoisting that 30-pound backpack onto her small shoulders and unconditioned backside just before hiking into the bowels of The Grand Canyon...

You are one crazy brave woman.

You are also about to reshape your life, your bones, and your pride.

Consider this: During the hike, you will weep in public because this is Pain, and it earns it's capitol P with interest. Like clockwork every hour, you will scream in your head, "This is not what I signed up for!" You will resist the Pain, the overloaded f-ing backpack, the endless number of steps, the Pain, the freeze-dried packets of food crap, and then there's the Pain.

You will discover that your expensive REI hiking shirt—the one with the thin "miracle fabric" that keeps you warm in cold weather and cool in hot weather—still makes you look fat no matter what the weather.

So why do this? If this hurts more than childbirth without meds, why choose a hike into a massive hole in the earth as your first "vacation" in a hundred years?

For the free gifts, of course!

Count on adding these to your canyon tote bag as you exit the South Rim:

• Company of Angels

You will discover you are hiking not only with old friends, but with unexpected companions who suddenly materialize. They show up at odd moments. It could happen when your friends hike far ahead as darkness falls and you are still miles from camp. Or maybe it happens when part of the trail is washed away by rain and you must crawl across the thinnest line of rock to avoid falling 6,000 feet. Somehow you make it to camp in darkness, and you skip the free-fall tour of the canyon.

The trail you are on is named Bright Angel for a reason. Stay alert for this gift, my friend.

• Solitude

Towering ancient rock walls offer silence to a noise-drenched modern world. This stillness magically helps even the most troubled of hearts. Bathe in this; let it treat the wounds. Keep this gift and practice canyon silence when you need to quiet a blathering inner, or outer, world.

• Surrender

Not a gift you're dying to have? Sorry, the canyon won't take no for an answer. Besides, this may be the best gift you get for all your trouble.

The canyon's unyielding landscape will remind you of hardships in your own life. How familiar are the never-ending series of uneven steps; the constant push to keep moving no matter how much you want to stop and rest. And despite all that grueling exertion, you will still look fat in that REI shirt.

Surrender seems crazy at a time like this, but resistance feels like war, with every rock and stone an enemy. You're outnumbered! Wave the white flag and get your free parting gift: A thrilling awareness of being alive and free in a beautiful world built by nature's grandest designer.

Storytelling feels like another artery extending from my heart. Stories flow from every experience. For years, as a newspaper journalist, I told the stories of others. Now I tell my own stories, either as fiction or nonfiction. It feeds my heart and makes me come alive.

SURRENDER

King Arthur's Cave
By Emma Hunter

When you are battle worn and exhausted to the marrow, follow in King Arthur's footsteps to his final resting place. Go into the woods where the beech canopy carves up sunlight into stippled glow. Go deeper into the darkest heart where trees grow thick. Take refuge inside the cave, just as Arthur did.

Meet the darkness. Let its cool air sooth your furied soul, let its mineral dew dampen your raging heart. Stand in the chapel chamber, all sound deadened by earth's pelvic bowl. Edge further still into the deepest recess, climb and squeeze yourself through unforgiving fissures of stone-carved musculature. Feel into that crawl space. Curl your weary body into that empty black nook.

Is it true? Did the Grail once lie here for safekeeping? Let the hairs on your skin come alive to the vibrations of its answer, echoing through time.

Extinguish your torch.

Feel what real darkness is. Feel its leathered wings fold themselves around you and sink you back into the silent black. Let the summer die.

Sleep.

Let the earth outside shift and remake itself so that your only exit aligns to one precise degree. Wait for the tilt, when the winter days grow desperately short. May you be woken before dawn, on solstice day, by a faint glimmer painted on the chamber wall; the seeping in of dawn's pre-emptive glow. Let this be the gentlest of stirrings; let the gatekeeper moths begin to gather. Slow and steady, may it grow your yearning strong enough that you may heave the winter sun out across the milky horizon.

And when that first chink of light splits through the last membrane of darkness, its searchlight beam begins its steady sweep across the cave walls, opening the dark by increments, to dilate your soul.

Your shadow:
haloed.

Do not be afraid. Surrender. Uncup your hands. Show the wick of your broken heart that it may catch the flame of Brigid's solstice fire. For one infinitesimal slice of time, drown in the deluge of a light so full that it sears through the cord that tied you to the dark.

In your moment of blindness, may you finally see.

And when the wheel of light has swept through the cave and on, and the after-glow wanes, be astonished at your own ignition.

Hollowed out,
confronted by the light,
see the chalice of your heart,
now forever lit.

Emma Hunter spends most of her life lost down all sorts of rabbit holes, bewilderedly searching for the answers to life's impossibly big questions. Sometimes she writes her findings down. Sometimes she makes drawings of them. Other times she just eats cake and stares out of the window.

Remember
By Pat Johnson

Just under the surface I see you there.
Just behind the door I hear you moving.

One last kick, you'll break the surface.
One more step, you'll come to the door.

Can you see the sunlight streaming?
Can you hear my voice calling you home?

Reach for that light.
Reach for that handle.

I know that your lungs are ready to burst.
I know that your legs are ready to collapse.

You've been swimming for way too long.
You've been running so very far.

You are an Olympic swimmer.
You are a Marathon runner.

Yet even whales come up for air.
Yet even runners take time to walk.

Know that I'll help you into the boat.
Know that I'll be there for you to lean on.

For I too have swum to the bottom of that ocean.
For I too have run to the end of the world.

Feel the fresh air in your lungs.
Feel the comfort of a resting place.

You've tried for so long, to save them from drowning.
You've tried so long, to keep them from getting lost.

But you forgot to breathe.
But you forgot to rest.

Let me help you remember.
For you are loved and not alone.

How to Survive a Rip Current (And Other Life Crises)
By Annie Ferguson Muscato

You'll find yourself caught in it before you can figure out what happened. Here is all you need to remember: don't panic. I know that's easier said than done, but try to relax. The good news is that the current is strongest near the surface, so it's not pulling you under, just out. And out won't kill you. The salt will carry your weight just as well in fifty feet of water as in five.

Eventually a wave will come crashing over you, filling your nostrils with burning salt water and disorienting you as it pushes you down. When it does, surrender to it and let it pull you under. I know we just talked about staying on the surface because under can kill you, but there is no point in sugarcoating this: under CAN kill you. But it won't if you don't let it.

Take a breath if you can. If you can't, resist the urge to inhale and trust that the oxygen already in your lungs is enough. The wave is a weight class above you and you're going into this fight tired, so don't waste energy fighting to the surface, you will only lose. Go against your instincts and dive down instead. The surface is where the hardest churning is, the sort that will fling you around like a rag in a washing machine. Dive down as far as you can to where it is still. Ride it out before you push back up.

After you catch your breath, take a rest. I know you think there is no time for it, but you'll need your strength to get out of this, so give yourself a break. Spread yourself over the surface, fill your lungs with buoyant air.

Once you have caught your breath it's time to get yourself back to shore. Like diving down to avoid a wave, the solution is counterintuitive. The current is pulling you out, but it will turn and slow down. Wait for the turn, and then swim at an angle back towards dry land. You won't be able to get back to where you started, but you'll get somewhere, and the sand there will seem warm, maybe even inviting.

More waves will come as you make your way, but remember they come in sets. Count them if you don't believe me, and you'll see. This too shall pass. And with each wave the dive down gets easier. Soon, you'll start to find comfort in the quiet of the ocean floor.

Rest. Move forward. Repeat. When you reach the beach you'll be exactly where you need to be.

Annie is a southern wife, mom, professional, graduate student, and wanna-be farmer. She resides in North Florida with her husband, Derek, daughter, Ellie Jo, and son, JP, on a horse farm at the end of a long dirt road. She finds joy in writing, early morning trail rides, perfectly made mint juleps, making her children laugh, cooking for a crowd, and southern colloquialisms.

Surviving the Abyss of Infancy
By Emily Rosen Rittenberg

Dear Mama,

These days are the longest you've ever experienced, but you can't get a thing done. You nurse until your nipples bleed and lie on your bed, comatose to the new reality, and the baby cries again. You look at the calendar and have a guilty moment of thinking about going back to work—a physical representation of your old life. You think, "maybe I was made without a maternal instinct like all the other moms." Your body will be fragile from the birth, the exhaustion of a newborn, the insanity of taking care of an entirely new human life. And you will be permanently different.

But look around for signs of normalcy. The way your creamer billows in your cup of coffee to the most beautiful swirl the world has ever made. How the warm water drip drops off your fingertips after you clean the dishes for the third time in the day. The forever hum of the lights as you numbly embrace your freedom to go to the grocery store at any time.

And in those moments you can find a peaceful magic no one teaches you about in birthing classes or doctors' appointments. An alchemy of awareness. A clarity of your tired senses, a calmness to your thoughts that are about the most basic of needs. An ok-ness to the new normal.

Be gentle to yourself. The only thing your tiny human needs is you—fully, authentically, essentially you.

Let go of the imaginary stories you tell yourself about how this should be, it will be what it will be.
Let go of your need to control how this will unfold, it will blossom at exactly the right moment.
Let go for your desire to capture this perfect moment on camera, submit to the perfection of presence.
Let go of your attachment to the narrative of who you were, you are new again.
Let go of the schedule that tells you that your new human is already doing it wrong, make up your own version of right.

No one will tell on you.

And in this dissolution of the self you once knew, you get back to how you started: *perfect*. Exactly what the universe needs you to be and exactly who your baby came to for guidance on this planet.

Embrace the chaos because in this stimulus you can choose how you will respond. Live your wisdom—it is infinite, it is powerful, and it is forever present, waiting for you to trust.

With light and love,
You

Emily Rosen Rittenberg, M.Ed. NCC, is a Parent Coach who helps parents with the normal but challenging problems they are facing with their kids and teens. She hosts in-person and online classes for parents on topics such as Nurturing Intrinsic Motivation, Emotion Coaching With Your Children, and Mindfulness for Parents. She lives in Rochester, NY with her husband and two children.

To Free My Captive Soul
By Deanna De Paoli

The Captors of my Soul did ransom seek,
My treasures and my wealth they did demand,
Caged and abandoned, they left me so weak,
On knees I cried out, for I could not stand.

My worth and value they sought as payment,
Everything that was outside my control,
With all my money and resources spent,
I could not find the way to make me whole.

My Heart spoke out to claim my Soul's release,
Placed me on the path that would set me free,
In full surrender I could find true peace,
I just had to breathe and let myself be.

From depths below to vast skies up above,
I freed myself when I accepted Love.

Creative Synthesizer—writer, lawyer, yogini exploring the synthesis of spirituality, law, and energy dynamics. Nourishing hearts, minds, and bellies. Sparking a movement to reclaim the Spirit of the Law.

When There's a Monster in the Abyss
By Linda Jackson

This thing. This habit. This situation.

That feels impossible.

That cannot be. That should not be.

This thing:

   It just is.

It is itself. It isn't you.

Let it be. As it is, in this moment.

It doesn't need to be any other way, just now.

No need to hide with it in the dark, skittering with wild eyes.

Shine the light. It's ok.

See it, as itself.

Seeing it releases it – to relax, or move.

Oh curious thing!

Greet it, and feel the calm in your body.

The soft release into the present.

You are not this thing, that is on its own journey.

You are beloved.

Aphorisms on Writing and Life
By Kris Bell

Love told me to
curl myself around my bones and rest,
to let my mind walk outside to the porch
and have a cigarette
and let my soul fly out the window.

Love told me to have
a blithe disregard for absolutes,
to try and keep God amused
and to sometimes eat cherry pie for breakfast.

Love told me that wealth
is not dependent on possessions
any more than wisdom is dependent on books
or education.

Love told me to
go about life and writing
in the same way an ant
goes about pushing and pulling
a boulder sized crumb up a hill;
without doubt or despair
or any worry as to whether or not it was
doing it right.

Love told me
to have patience with myself,
that I'm just beginning,
that I am a long blooming flower
and not to rush the process
to remember that it takes a billion
years to form a precious jewel.

Love told me that
when I run out of things to say
I could pause and have tea with hedgehogs
or work on a revised edition
of *What Color are Your Spots:*
A Career Guide for Appaloosas, Dalmatians,
Leopards and Bush Snakes.

Love told me that
no matter what I do
one day death will come
in my sleep, just like I had
always hoped and that I might as well
at least jot down a few notes here
and there, even if it's just chicken scratch.

Love told me that we put our
heroes on a pedestal right up there
with God, not to make ourselves small
but because in time we
mean to measure up.

Love told me to
go out to the playground
after dark, when it's empty,
to close my eyes
and beckon the childhood
that blew away one day on the
wind and drifted slowly across the sky
like a golden leaf in autumn.

Love told me not to try
so hard, just write about anything
at all...the color of your grief
or the way wild elephants
stand silently over the bodies of
their dead companions and
stroke their sun bleached bones
as if gathering memories.

Kris is a wife, mother, way finder, soul tender, spiritual seeker and blossoming writer.
She lives in a cozy house in California with her husband and two children.

(Im) Patience
By Anna Bruk

This poem was inspired by a clock designed by Debbie Millman. Over the years, it has become a friend in the moments when Time seems to be a torturer rather than healer, constantly reminding of its designer's wisdom: "Expect anything worthwhile to take a long time".

I beg you'd move faster,
Stop, go back.
Anything but this.

And all you say in return is:
Now. Now. Now.
Tick fucking tock.

I fume, roar, and despair
While you march forward
Unapologetically, whispering

That surrender to what is
Is just around the corner,
In every now, if I choose so,

Yet, still making known
It's ok that getting there
Will take a long time.

Anna Bruk is a perpetual seeker of light who, after 30 years, finally called off the search party, picked up a pen (well, technically the notes app in her phone), and let the light come to her. Her writing is fueled by curiosity, love of paradox, and simple carbohydrates.

Chaos
By Crystal Pirri

Everything is chaos before we understand it.

Think of the things we've assumed were chaos —
"Here be dragons" on our earliest maps,
billions of stars in random clusters,
even the chance existence of our own rock
slowly gliding around the dented table
of gravity created by this solar system.
Truly, the more we understand a thing
the less we see its chaos
and begin to see its beauty.

Hold this in your heart
the next time you feel uncertain.
Surrender to the unknowing
and underneath your surrender
know only this:
this is something bigger
and more beautiful
than you can yet fathom.
And it loves you,
supports you,
and cares for you
the way gravity cradles your soft body
on this Earth.

Crystal Pirri is an author, coach, and founder of programs that help women become free. Her cutting-edge book on habits was taught at Kent State University, and her coaching has helped women create businesses, increase their income, and completely change their lifestyles to become the women they want to be. Connect with her at http://CrystalPirri.com.

You are the Horse.
By Jennifer Shryock

You are the horse.

Your soul, your invisible rider,
presses her knee
gently to your side.
At first you ignore it.
You've got big plans,
work to do,
expectations.
Her knee guides toward an unclear path,
an invitation.

Of course you may decline, dearest.
Stay your course,
hold to the familiar.

Or surrender your certainty,
break the rules,
abandon your earnest intentions
for the mystery you want even more.

Your invisible rider gently presses her knee.

After years of climbing the proverbial career ladder instead of the Rocky Mountains,
Jennifer Shryock felt lost, sick. Against all odds and prognoses, illness guided her home
to a magical life helping others reconnect to their deepest nature, heal their careers, and
find and make their own magic.

TRANSFORMATION

The Becoming
By DK Crawford

This piece is dedicated to Miracle, the one-winged male monarch who chose to live with me for three weeks. By sharing his soul and journey with me, and relying on me to help him find food, he taught me how to have grace around my own transformation and how truly beautiful vulnerability can be.

I'm leaning on the edge, pushing gently. This elastic form yields to my body. Anyone looking from the outside would see shadows: my elbows and fingers probing the membrane. Expanding. Testing. What once felt like my prison is now my nest, holding me for a bit longer before I must fly.

I am an impatient fledgling, yearning for what more is out there. But my higher consciousness begs me to appreciate this time. This wiser part knows I will long for this season of becoming when I have flown.

I am not ready yet, but I am close.

I was terrified when I began to change. I screamed as darkness surrounded me and felt I would suffocate and die, but a voice spoke through the darkness, commanding me to trust. "Listen... This is how it must happen. Surrendering helps."

Yet I still fought as insanity flooded me and my existence narrowed to almost nothing. I was isolated in a silent, dark world—no longer a part of the life I'd known. My familiar form melted away and my cells began to rearrange themselves. I sat in the goo of nothingness I'd become and tried not to panic.

I was other.

Ancestral whispers sang to me in the darkness telling me stories of their own transformations. "You will come through this," they promised me. "Sometimes you need someone else to hold faith when you have lost your own. We are here to tell you, you will be OK." And then they were gone. Their occasional visits were my lifeline. They were proof that someone else had survived this passage.

Now I am mostly formed, though strengthening still. I see filtered light and shadows through the barrier around me. I hear caws of crows beckoning and smell salt breezes wafting. I am neither other, nor am I yet them, but I am finally, deeply, myself.

"Will I be able to sustain the me I have become?" "Will my wings unfold and dry as they should?" "Will I be able to fly, feed and follow the light to my new destination?" "Can I trust myself to hear my truth and act on my instincts?"

I didn't before, I pray I do now.

So many have gone before me and not come this far. Some never leave their original form. Some are struck down before they even crawl.

I am chosen.

I stretch again. My cocoon gives more than it ever has and light breaks through its raveling fabric. The voices circle again, "Easy… It's not time yet. Hold space for where you are in this moment. Relax into what is."

I stop pushing. I circle my folded wings around me and squeeze myself and inhale my saturated essence. Just as I long for freedom and adventure I also know I will miss the embrace of this incubatory home. I snuggle in and choose to love this time with myself a little bit longer. Flight will come soon enough.

DK Crawford is a writer and photographer who revels in her relationships with animals, plants and nature. She's enamored with beauty and witnesses tiny miracles every single day. She is currently in a transformation and learning to embrace her own becoming.

Miracle, the one-winged male monarch
By DK Crawford

Wingspan
By Noelle Newby

Trusting not the Chrysalis,
We craft our own cocoons.
Empty bottles,
Glowing screens,
All the short-lived glues.

Like a picture,
Love a tweet,
Buy the latest fad.
Don a bauble, and another,
Binge, repeat 'til mad.

Compare ourselves to all our friends,
For what they have we lack.
Grace and luck,
Wit and pluck,
Retreat, submit, attack.

Someday, someday, someday,
We'll be ready to take flight.
Someday, once we're done becoming,
And everything's *just right.*

Until a day, we cannot breathe
A single, free-felt breath.
Choking comfort,
Banished soul,
Up-and-coming death.

"You are enough," a whisper says,
In wait to amplify.
"Beyond enough, even more,
There's nothing left to try."

"Discard your shell of disbelief
And toddle into trust.
Gnaw and claw through silk and sand,
I'll wait beyond the dust."

"Weightless, dauntless
Strong and sound,
You're born to leap and sing.
It's time you know, without a doubt
The power in your wings."

Noelle is a writer, yogi, marketer, wife and a 40-something-year-old mother of two cherished children under the age of five. Instead of sleeping, she loves, writes, works, plays and thoroughly enjoys life in her hometown of Austin, Texas.

Cake
By Jenn Stuart

There is a plain brown egg warming in a bowl on the counter.
You know, we did not always keep our eggs in the fridge.
But, these days we're *so afraid*.
I heard that factory farming has found a way to put salmonella into the egg
itself, rather than just the chicken, so washing your egg won't absolve you.
The actual risk of *contamination* is small really, but who among us is willing to
risk it?
Also, a refrigerated egg lasts for two months whereas an egg on the counter
only lasts a week. Who has time these days to babysit an egg?
The taste and quality are inferior but nobody cares. Well, some of us do.
Those chilly eggs are too cool to participate in baking.
They would need to find a way to warm up first.

So anyway, an egg waits in a bowl, all alone, in a space between here and there.
It is slowly acclimatizing to its more temperate environment, losing its chill.
When the time comes, an egg will crack, altering it irreparably.
The inside will be on the outside! Which is where it must be in order to do some
good.
The thick gel-like albumen will slide out over the jagged edges of the shell,
protecting the dense nutrient-rich yolk as it slips into a new space.
The yolk is a sun, suspended, one of the only food sources of vitamin D.
How does the sunshine vitamin end up hidden so deep within a shell?

An egg is essential to baking.
If you beat an egg it changes form.
Whip in some air and it froths into foam, rich and light all at once.
Add other ingredients and the egg can bind them together,
emulsifying what was previously un-join-able.
Add heat and true magic occurs: a viscous batter will transform into something
Substantial.
It. Will. Rise. Up.

An egg can merge with the others and be reborn into oneness.
An egg can lose itself into the structure of this new thing.
It can be essential, integral and indivisible from the whole.
In baking, a new reality can form, delicious and sublime.
This good can be a divine sacrament, on offer to nourish us all.

For now an egg waits on the counter.
It is hoping it could be cake.

In the fall of 2017 a US Border Agent asked Jenn to state her profession. In years past she had stammered Student, then Student (still), then Student (again), then Designer (hmm), then Stay-at-home mom (sigh). But, this day she met his eye and declared: "Writer." And, so it was.

Three Wishes
By Paula Boone

Once upon a time there was a princess who had a very evil mother. This evil queen was jealous of anything good that happened for her daughter and tried to sabotage every relationship the princess had. Her mother took any opportunity to "put her in her place." The princess wasn't sure what that meant, but she knew it involved lots of criticism and name-calling.

The princess tried to make the evil queen happy, but nothing she did was ever good enough. So she willingly ate the poison apples the queen regularly fed her—they didn't kill her, at least not immediately, but instead filled her with poisonous negativity.

In desperation, she appealed to her father, the king, to intervene. This enraged the evil queen so much that she made everyone's life miserable.

One day the princess slipped out of the castle and sat beside a pond. She was looking at her own reflection when a frog hopped up beside her.

"Hello," he said.

"Hello," she answered.

"Do you need for me to kiss you?" she asked.

"Whatever for?" he asked.

"To turn you into a prince," she replied.

"I'm very happy being a frog," he said, "and anyway you don't seem very happy being a princess."

The princess told the frog about her mother and all the things she had come to believe about herself, how she was afraid her mother was right, that she was an ungrateful and selfish girl. She confessed how much she hated it when she saw herself being judgmental or biased. She admitted that her greatest fear was that she would turn out to be exactly like her mother and because of that fear, she seldom expressed her wants or needs.

"I'll tell you what," the frog said. "Make three wishes for your mother and then I will let you kiss me."

"Okay," she said.

1. I wish my mother used her power for good.
2. I wish my mother was kind and compassionate.
3. I wish my mother knew how to love and be loved.

"Done," said the frog.

"Just like that?" asked the princess.

"Just like that," said the frog.

The princess leaned down and kissed the frog and instantly she was turned into a frog. The two of them hopped off together and lived happily ever after.

The End.

Paula aspires to be creative in all things. She splits her time between her home in South Carolina and traveling with her husband in their motor home. Izzy, a seven-year-old schnauzer, is her constant companion and doorbell.

Once Upon a Game of Chess
By Dr. Irina Kotlar

The Game was about to begin. The pieces rushed to their places but a little Dark Pawn lingered, enchanted by the radiating presence of the Light Queen.

The Queen grasped the Pawn's look.

"Let's talk before the Game. You know you can end up where I begin…"

"But…"

"Sure, usually Pawns get sacrificed near the start and…don't make it across the board.

But! Only Pawns have a special ability—if you reach the opponent's side of the board you can transform yourself into any other piece. Such is the alchemy of the Game.

Get to my place of power and help the Game. That Path is riddled with dangers at every move. But there are no sheltered Paths on the board.

Remember, if you have a desire, there is a place for you and you'll be supported. Find the safest path. Keep your eyes on where you want to be."

"I have to defend…"

"There are more powerful pieces in defense, that make seemingly more impressive moves than you. Your true power begins on the opposite side of the board.

The Light start leading the Game. Played right, they win. The Dark either react or accept the invitation to a strong, creative counter-play. When the Light lose initiative the Dark can outsmart them.

Every Pawn has the power to become a Queen. I find it strange that Pawns rarely walk that path.

Remember, your every move matters. Go!"

The Game began. The Pawn started on her long journey. Her team counted her as lost. Pawns rarely get across the board.

She went on, fighting her way. Alone and scared, she focused on that one place—the place of power.

Getting there the Pawn turned round. The Dark were losing. The Light lost their Queen as they focused on decisive attack.

"You made it… I didn't think you would…" said the off-the-board Queen.

"You told me???"

"Everybody is going to leave the Game eventually — there is nothing to lose, why not dare? The Dark could have lost had you not transformed into the powerful Queen. Go help them now."

And she did. The Dark were as surprised as the Light when the Pawn — now the Queen — unexpectedly blitzed across the board, scrambled the attack and stood in defense of her King. The Game ended in a draw.

"Why did you help me? We're enemies," said the Pawn to the Queen as the pieces were taken back to the box.

"I'm the strongest piece in the Game. When I'm out, a courageous and wise piece has to keep the Game on. Everyone perfects their game, and the next, and the whole Game of Chess evolves.

There is an illusion of two teams. In reality, we fight to make each other A stronger and the Game worthwhile.

Thank you for making the journey."

"Thank you for giving me faith. The Path gave me courage. A brief moment in your place gave me wisdom. I'll take it into the next Game."

Unexpectedly stumbling on an invisible something on a brightly lit Career Path, Irina suddenly found herself dropped into an underworld of spiritual journeys, illuminated only by the faint light of a blind faith, while the alternative Sun might be rising on a horizon on the other side of the Earth.

Life as a Zero Sum Game
By Amanda Chudak

Please help me to see
that there is no gain,
just change,
that there is no loss,
just change,
and, in this way,
become the joy of each moment.

Amanda Chudak knows very little about anything, but sometimes she likes to imagine she does. The results range from serendipitous to painfully banal. She rewards herself with chocolate either way.

I Am Curious
By Marion Perepolkin

As a young girl I am curious.
I wander into a golden field.
I stand in the field and sense the field in me.
Golden grasses, golden hair.
Bluest skies, bluest eyes.
Witness and stillness.

As an adolescent I am curious.
Cherry orchard, ripened fruit.
A ladder...I climb and perch on top.
I am enveloped in evening's attire,
a golden pink sunset.
Witness and stillness.

As an adult I am curious.
A drive across land to the ocean
to make a move, take a leap.
I feel like a shorebird who has
found her abundance.
I relax, I write and paint...forever changed,
forever the same.
Witness and stillness.

Currently I am coming full circle in my life. I did in fact move to the West Coast after a long absence. After much life experience, travel and the writing of my memoir, I am exploring possibilities. T.S. Eliot's quote is ringing true for me. I have arrived where I started from and feel I know the place for the first time.

Three Stillnesses
By Shelby Bach

1.
The fall is unforgiving.
The impact jars your bones.
The bare rock scrapes the skin
from your palms and knees.

This pit is deep,
dark and slick with damp.
There's no way out,
save the way you came,
too high to reach.
You want to call for help, but
these stones swallow words.

You are lost until
the moon rises, generous with light.

Standing at the wall's base,
you study its cracks and divots.
You pick a path and
begin to climb
on tender, trembling limbs.

Halfway up, you glance down
to see how far you've come.
Footprints of blood stain
the circumference of the cave—
your own.

Without words, you cannot lie, even to yourself.

One wound predates the fall:
Your soles are shredded
from all the scurrying you've done
to chase the whims of the world.
You've left your own damage
trailing in your wake.

2.
The second time, the entrance is wider.
Perhaps that's why
you tumble into the hole
you diligently skirted for years,
or perhaps you were too busy
cursing the sky for your dead beloved
to attend to the ground beneath your feet.

The cave welcomes you,
its bare stone now wrapped with
a cushion of moss, a soft sanctuary
for you and your aching heart.

You wait.
The moon rises, generous with light,
and brightens the path.
You don't climb yet.
The world didn't have room for your pain.

Stones swallow words, but moss drinks tears.

You stay and feel enough
pain until briefly,
you find its end and uncover
the love that shivers underneath.

3.
The predator howls, and
as fear trumpets,
your heart remembers the cave.

The moss soothes your raw soles.
The moon rises, generous with light,
and illuminates the saplings around you—
a forest in miniature on the cavern floor.

The predator's shadow falls across the entrance,
but he cannot follow you to your solitary sanctuary.
You cannot leave—trapped, with only
your own voice for company.

Stones swallow words, but they don't stopper song.

You indulge in a few notes, a brief musical phrase,
longing only to hear the echo.
Instead, you receive notes in a higher key—
Farther off, another voice sounds, offering its own phrase,
then another, and another,
rising from other wordless caverns nearby,
threaded like veins under the surface of the world.

Every singer offers what notes they can,
a small contribution in the hope of a greater melody.
Even the predator's distant howl has a place,
but his wail is the saddest phrase of all
in a symphony ringing with bottomless joy.

Shelby Bach never considered herself a poet—at least until she joined the Write into Light course. There, inspired by the luminescent work of her fellow writers, Shelby wrote mostly verse for months on end. (She has since wondered if poetry borrowed her hands and wrote itself. Verdict? Completely possible.)

Cold Floors and Blueberry Bread
By Becky Flynn

From the loneliest place you can imagine
will come the greatest love you have
ever
ever
known

From a sweating
shaking
insomnia-filled
mess
on a cold kitchen floor
will rise a warrior

When there is no possibility left
in your soul
you will hope for nothing
and then
then
receive everything

Hand over your heart
bloody and blackened

You think
all you'll get in exchange
is
pity
rage
guilt
equally measured agony

But what you'll get instead
is
Warm blueberry bread
A soft blanket
A big spoon-sweeping embrace
An "I love you"

A way through
A way home

Social worker. Mental health advocate. INFJ enigma. Tortoise not the hare. Yogi. Bumbling Poet.

Between Worlds
By Liz Wiltzen

You've galloped, heart leading, across the open plain toward your destiny; wisdom your quest, truth your battle cry, courage your steed.

And now you have arrived at the threshold of the known, the place where the seen and unseen meet. This is the passage between worlds. Flight beckons—do you hear its call?

Feel your feet curling into talons; clenching the earth, seeking something to hold onto, something certain, something known.

Feel your limbs transforming into wings, yearning to reach higher realms of seeing.

Listen to your soul, as the breeze rustles one delicate feather tip, telling you it's time. This is the updraft of the ancestors, the wisdom that has travelled between worlds to lift you.

Transcending gravity, you must harness your keen vision to pierce through illusion. Pay attention. Shadow becomes darkest as it approaches the light.

As you trust your wings and begin to soar, riding thermals of Love to the heavens, danger will appear in your path. You will come under attack from an enemy within, one that sees only Earth; does not believe in Sky. Sees your quest as predator; itself as prey.

Shifting its shape, it will use Sky against you; become the fierce winds, the thunder and lighting, the driving rain. Emerging from your own fear of darkness, it will thrust a claw skyward to steal you from flight. Wrapping itself around your life force, it will tear—if you let it—one feather at a time from your sacred wings, and hurl your shattered body back to the earth below.

Breathe. Drop into the still space between heartbeats. Feel the Love that you are.

This evil cannot claim you. It does not own you. It has no power here.

You are no longer girl. You are Hawk.

You came to kiss the earth with your magnificent wing tips, and to soar above it, seeing all. A magic cauldron of Hawks, each one adding voice to the cast, has been waiting for you to join them.

You belong Here.
You belong to Earth and Sky.

Now Hawk

Now Wind
Now Sky
Now Air

You belong to the Seen and the Unseen.

You were born to move between worlds, and to share what you see.

*For me, writing is a way of finding words to capture the intriguing meaning in the
events of life, and then creatively arranging those words in a way that delights and
inspires. After a long sabbatical, I have started publishing my writing again on my blog
and Medium.com:*
http://liveattuned.com/blog
https://medium.com/@lizwiltzen

Starry Night
By Liz Wiltzen
Watercolor
14 x 21 inches

Mystery
By Amanda Cooke

Mystery,
Make me an instrument of the Unseen.
Guide me between worlds.
I long to know the wild edge of life.

For too long my heart was the prisoner of my mind,
Until I dared taste your offerings of freedom.

I am ready now,
To be a student of Truth,
To learn the tongues of the Cosmos,
To interpret the stories of the seeds germinating in the womb of my soul.

Mystery,
I feel your benevolent winds at my back, and yet,
I am still afraid.

Grant me the courage to roam the vast empty plains in search of truth, with the
faith that I will never be lost.

Grant me the fearlessness to experience the fullness of love knowing that I also
risk feeling its inextricable loss.

Grant me the compassion to hold all parts of myself tenderly, and the grace to
offer mercy to those who are not yet ready to love all of themselves.

Grant me the serenity to see that even in the chaos I will always have the
compass of my soul.

Grant me the humility to know that I am but one drop, and the wisdom to know
that I am also the whole ocean.

Mystery,
Make me an instrument of the Unseen.
Show me the way Home.

Amanda is a writer who spent the last six years living and organic farming in the
Australian wilderness where she reconnected with nature and herself. She now lives
with her family on a houseboat in Amsterdam. Read more of Amanda's work on:
https://www.theclearingonline.com/amanda-bio-page.

By Amanda Cooke

RENEWAL

Sestina: When we were young and green
By Elizabeth Spelman

When we were young and green, we reached out and touched the leaves on
either side of the path.
Our mud-squeezed toes fled the cricketing heat of the long meadows to hide in
the green
Woods. We hunted frogs along the river until we saw the afternoon light change
And ran home for dinner. The dinner was a sacrifice
To placate the gods, who let us fall, with our mosquito-bitten legs and fruit-
ripened stomachs, asleep,
Without a bath, our bodies covered in dirt.

When we were older, we dyed our hair blonde and wore St. John suits. At the
first sign of dirt
We went to the cleaners, driving on a road cut so wide that the edges of the
path
Disappeared on the horizon. Driving on a road like that asleep
Is easier than you might think. We washed away our green-
Stained fingers and mud-brown toes and made our bed-time rituals into a
sacrifice
To a god who demanded we drive, asleep, on a road that would never, with the
seasons, change.

Into the toll booths along this road, we threw our change,
Hard-earned by working, although not in the dirt.
We were unaware of the sacrifice
We made to drive on such a wide path. A path
We would never have chosen when we were young and wanted our hands to
turn green
Before we fell asleep.

When we were older, we let our hair turn gray. We fell asleep
In our easy chair with our feet propped up on the hassock; We would remotely
change
The channel. Our hands were blue, and they twisted more than the garlands we
once wove out of green
Ivy growing in the root-rich dirt. Dirt
That washed from the fields into the eutrophicated river at the end of the
narrow path
Along which we once ran, as the afternoon sun, gloaming into evening, sank,
into the river — a sacrifice.

What a blessing it is, to still see a gold-dust sunset after all these years. I would not willingly sacrifice
Another twilight to the blue flicker of the black-top road. When I fall asleep,
I am alive. When I am awake, I am at rest. I have found again the narrow path
On which my wide-open arms feel the shiver of a breeze in the leaves. Leave me here. No change
Is as necessary as letting the jungle overtake the road, so the dirt
Can turn my feet, once again, mud-brown, and I can feel, once again, what it is to be young, with fingers stained green.

We want you to be young and green.
Safe in a world in which sacrifice
And blessing grow from the same dirt.
Safe in a world in which you fall asleep
In the murmuring fields, one arm shielding your eyes. The change
Is not in the toll booths. It fell onto the dirt of the narrow path.

Look at us, digging in the dirt to find change. Good. We will find it everywhere along the path.
We will find it in the dark woods, in the green fields, along the quiet river, and in the gold sunset we watch together before we fall asleep.
Let us make a sacrifice to the gods at twilight. Let us thank them for giving us change.

I am an architect currently living in Phoenix, Arizona.

For Everything There Is A Season
By Julianne May

Stumbling and breathless, I ran from the storm until I became entangled in the roots of the undergrowth. Had I been running for days or years? Brushing myself off, I noticed the ground was littered with debris from the thick canopy. Tendrils of wild vines summoned me beyond the sentinel oaks, ancient guardians of this place where time held no governance but for everything there is a season.

Hunger tugged in my belly and my throat prickled dry. I couldn't get my bearings without a clear view to the sun.

A magpie came into sight but seemed too busy shuffling through the understory on a foraging mission to notice me. My heart sank to see her wings were broken. As I moved forward she disappeared at light speed. A sharp point tapped at my heel and a musical voice broke the silence —

"Why did you chase me"?

I replied, "I hoped to mend your wings"

The magpie released a joyous song.

"Show me no pity, these legs are strong, I move fast and I receive all I need from the forest floor". She then chortled gently, "You look tired; let my wings comfort you while you rest".

When I woke, shafts of sunlight ignited trails throughout the forest. The magpie had left a pile of berries and blanketed me beneath the largest leaves from an ancient oak tree.

As I stretched, a yellow-eyed tortoiseshell cat, previously camouflaged by the shadows, materialised. Her double-bass purring commanded my attention.

"Where did you come from"? I asked.

"Everywhere, nowhere. It doesn't matter, I'm here now".

The velvet sound continued, "The real question is why are *you* here"?

"I don't know my way out".

"Oh, you're lost".

One drop at a time, tears began to fall. As I wept, the water quickly gathered enough momentum to forge a river. The cat slipped between my legs in a series of figure eights, purring so loudly my heart surrendered to her hypnotic rhythm. Leaping onto a high branch, her saucer eyes reflected limitless galaxies, while the forest whispered, *We have been waiting for you forever. Look, the seedlings are blooming along the river bank.*

All around wildflowers sprang up in revival, and although the cat was no longer at the scene, my still heart moved to her purring rhythm. I cupped my hands to quench my thirst in the crystal water. It tasted of liberation as it washed through my system.

I drew my first deep breaths in forever, buoyantly rising with the fragrant breeze. Floating even higher, I became suspended above the forest floor until a flock of rainbow lorikeets elevated my featherweight body high amongst the treetops. Sunlight warmed my being as I continued to rise above the canopy only to dissolve magnificently into the atmosphere. In wild conspiracy with nature, millions of my glistening particles descended in delicate spirals.

When the seed from my centre finally came to rest, it nestled deep in the warm earth knowing that, now, I had everything I needed to bloom again.

Julianne May is seeking to understand who she is in this world. As an apprentice in creative alchemy she consciously allows her curiosity to lead her down rabbit holes of "research." She spends too much time dreaming and not enough time doing. One day if fortune shines on her, she will have a dog of her own to love unconditionally.

By Cynthia Rome

Lying Fallow
By Carol Finch

The surface of the ground lies barren. Frozen, cracked, uneven. Not a blade of grass. Neither flowers nor fruit. A vast expanse of nothingness, as far as the eye can see, meeting the horizon and merging with the sky.

Such contrast to the perpetual activity of above, where clouds collide and worlds of images appear and disappear across the heavens. Such emptiness, such aloneness, an occasional fox punctuating the stillness.

My Love, know that it will not always be like this. What looks like death holds a universe of possibility.

What you see as inactivity, indecision, confusion and apathy is in fact a giant cosmos bursting with aliveness and potential creativity. Lying fallow does not equal nothing, quite the contrary.

Beneath the surface life is at work, laying down roots, strengthening intentions, holding a nurturing space for past hurts to be integrated and then transmuted into the very fabric of the soil.

Soil from which will emerge new shoots of hope and movement, impulses and desires. And as the new life grows it covers the ground with a colourful carpet—millions of species of interacting, entwining, interconnected cogs of a world where each strand is playing its part in a magnificent orchestra.

Be patient, My Love. In doing nothing you are being everything. Allow time to play its part and when you are ready you will emerge once again, ready to share your magic with the world.

An explorer of what it is to be a human, being. Using photography, writing, art and my love of the natural world. www.aspacetobe.com

And Yet
By Leslie K Sullivan

Adore Haydn's unfinished symphony.
Why doubts inhabit your evolving art?
Third act of Drood old dusty mystery
Is solved with audience democracy.
Each life its own Winchester mystery curse
Great vision overcomes mind's inward eye.
We share address; create a universe
A rooming house with inspiration high.
New easily comes; why yearn adoration?
Springboard from past reflects our human ties.
With reprise, arts' self finds consummation
Creations enlightening opens allies.
Plié, sketch, sing, act, write, sculpt, jump rein-free,
Remake with joy! Bold possibility.

Leslie Sullivan works in banking as a system and project manager. She holds degrees in Communication (with emphasis on oral interpretation of literature) and Industrial Engineering. During non-work hours, Leslie devotes time to her significant other and her extended family. She also studies voice, reads, and is handmaiden to resident cat, Princess Widget.

Changing Frequencies
By Angela Housley

Remember when radios were the main source of music. They have two knobs—one big, one little—that you rotate. As you turn, a red needle moves across a number line. As it moves, you hear white noise, but then something happens and you catch a recognizable sound. Fingers twist, the ear strains, and the brain hones in for more information.

Inexperienced users make big turns and stop when they hear music. Seasoned radio listeners operate very differently. The minute white noise turns into audible sound, the fingers shift from making big twists to infinitesimal ones. It's the heart that decides whether to stay and listen or move on.

The heart knows what the heart knows.

I realize now that the dynamic quality of the radio was its manualness. When you turn it on, if you don't like the station, you move the dial. You don't think about other things. Your ears, your mind, your heart all work together to find that which will spark joy.

Are you enjoying the station you are listening to now?

There is always another station out there. Yes, the white noise will not be comfortable. But go ahead. Start twisting the knobs. It's time.

Angela Housley is a lifelong soul searcher. While living as an expat in Hiroshima, Japan, she found her writer's voice.

Discovering Recovery
By Laurie Swanson

I see you carry your hamster wheel
It's a lot like the wheel I used to have
I feel the weight of it
The love and the hate of it

I see your hands gripping so tightly
It's a lot like the grip I used to have
I feel the fear in it
The far and the near of it

I see the hopelessness in your eyes
It's a lot like the look I used to have
I feel the pain of it
The loss and the gain of it

I see the glimmer of light you hold
It's a lot like the flame I used to have
I feel the hope of it
The noose and rope of it

I see resolve entering your heart
It's a lot like what I finally have
Feel the power of it
The here and now of it

Live in constant rediscovery
Don't give up on your recovery

An optimistic, knowledgeable and resourceful career coach and recruiter, Laurie Swanson is on a mission to advance the careers of women in Information Technology, thereby closing the wage gap and bringing feminine qualities into IT leadership. Also known as saving the world.

The Permission Slip
By Kim Brahm Oswald

Amongst the ashes of certainty's collapse,
The embers of possibility smolder.
Stand still in this discomfort that you are convinced
Shouts of your blazing un-belonging.

Don't waste energy chasing the sunrise.
Sit in the black of night and breathe.
You didn't have to ask to be sacred.
You just had to show up.

Dichotomy will dissolve
And drip through your bones.
Your vigilant watchman may rest.
You were never meant to be unbreakable.

Grant yourself permission
To repeatedly shatter in rawness.

Fall apart so the angels can find
And carry each piece of you.
They will rebuild a living mosaic
Of divine love temporarily housed in human flesh.

When you inevitably emerge,
Rearranged, light reflective, and nuanced,
Press this permission slip
Into the next palm amidst collapse.

Rain on the Windscreen
By Clare Allen

Born Anew
By Naina Saligram

Fragments of Pentelic marble once formed the temple of Athena Nike.
There used to be a statue here, forty feet tall,
Towering above mortals and covered in gold.
Now, the archeological ruin lies crumbled, covered in grime.

I pray not to Athena today, nor to Saraswati, nor to Isis —
Goddesses of wisdom, though they may be.
I sacrificed myself at their altars for too long.
What good did it do me?

Today, I call out to you, Kali.
Fierce Kali. Mother Kali.
Embodiment of opposition:
Protector and Destroyer, both.

Kali, do not shield me any longer.
I submit to the elements willingly.
Scorch me to ashes; break me with the wind.

Kali, she who means "black,"
Devour me with darkness.
Plunge me into the Ganges and let me drown.

Kali, she who means "time,"
Erase the memories of who I was,
For I am her no longer.

Kali, wife of Shiva,
Take an axe to the rubble and banish it to dust.
Strangle me whole with your ten arms.

Kali, motive agent of the karmic cycle,
Let the past go, so the future can rise.
Let me die, so I can be born.

The storm has passed, but the wreckage remains.
They say I'm in a period of Deep Recovery.
But what is left to recover? Can the fragments be pieced together?

This is not a restoration.
This is not a revival.
This is Creation itself.

Kali, purest representation of Brahman, the universe, of all there is —
Here I am,
Prostrate before you.

And I pray,

Make me whole.

Make me new.

Naina Saligram is a question-asker and truth-seeker who often finds herself pondering the complexities of subjectivity, time, beauty, and other Big Ideas. Her favorite things are words and images, usually in conjunction with one another.

In Between
By Susan A. Ring

To die is like being born, a new world.
Liminal light space divides us now. I let go.

My body left behind, death imminent, breath caught between.
It's not my time. Abundant life left to live.
Be still. Remember, death is not goodbye.

Love holds all, here and there.
Consciousness revealed in our stars.
Look to the eyes, colored stardust home.

Susan A. Ring is the author of <u>*The Unexpected Mother*</u> *and* <u>*When Hope Becomes Life.*</u>

Born into Death, and Gentle Illumination
By Jeana Bird

The driver didn't see the other deer. The woman watched from the edge of the woods as the car slowed to miss one deer, then shot forward again. The woman's stomach lurched. Her quiet walk came to crashing catastrophe. It was the worst death she had ever witnessed.

The car hit with such force that it gutted the deer on the spot. Abdomen split, one thrashing body in the road, one separate pile of innards. The woman's body stood rigid, burning like a bolt of lightning frozen in a photograph.

As the deer's death throes slowed, the woman's eyes turned. The gut pile had started to thrash. She stepped close. She saw twin fawns, smeared, wet and wincing as their one wild life came and went in a matter of seconds. Born into Death. So thin and long they looked. All legs and neck and spine.

She walked toward the car. A torrent of judgment viciously tore into her mind, shielding her grief. She clenched her jaw, trying to reject rage, her muscles a blockade of tension.

"STUPID CARS! STUPID HUMAN WORLD BLINDLY RUNNING OVER EVERYTHING!!!!!!!!!!!!!!!"

With each step toward the stunned driver, she yanked in her anger.

"SLOW DOWN!!! DOESN'T ANYONE KNOW WHERE THERE IS ONE DEER, THERE'S PROBABLY ANOTHER?"

The thoughts came, and she shoved them down. The driver rolled down her window.

"Is my bumper ok?"

The woman forced herself to speak with quiet reassurance. "Yes, it's ok. You go on ahead, I'll take care of the deer." The driver nodded with the gratitude of a hurried life being allowed to hurry along. The car sped away.

The woman heaved the mother deer off the road and gently carried the tiny twins to her side. After dark she returned to claim them. She buried the twins in a quiet place in the woods, a spot where she often went to sit and feel life.

She wondered, what could she have said? She craved connection and awareness. But her screaming judgments would not create connection; they would sever, blinding like a flash of light. Her own growing awareness has been a gentle illumination, gathering light like the dawn. And still, she made blind mistakes, achingly narrow in their flippant, fast focus.

She wondered how to speak what rage and grief want to speak. She wondered how she could do it without shame and blame. Or if there was some truth deeper than the feelings. The sun rising in the sky does not chase away the darkness, casting it out with self-righteous glare. It simply rises and shines, and the darkness fades away. Darkness does not fight the light, nor does light fight the darkness. The woman pondered how to learn that dance.

She began by working all morning to skin the mother deer, cutting up her flesh to feed life.

Jeana Bird lives on Waldron Island, WA where she grows food, writes poems and stories, plays fiddle and makes handmade shoes, walks through woods and on beaches, cultivates community, and studies and teaches MindBody integration skills. Her favorite activity is dreaming of ways to create healing and harmony in this life.

III.
CONNECTING

Photograph by Kelly Berg

REMEMBRANCE

Approaching Dust
By Michelle Wells

With each breath we are approaching dust.
Yet the trees whisper a love song, inviting us to dance.
Will we heed the call?

Perhaps it seems so hard for we are much too busy becoming.
Becoming what? Becoming who? Do we even know?
Does that part really matter at all?

You don't have to *be* anything to dance.
To show up and participate, without apology —
A tangled mess of arms and legs trying to recall the original rhythm of your
heart.

The trees will be gracious as we remember:
"It's never too late. There is no hurry.
We are only here to worship*".

Slide off your shoes and hold my hand: *"You are never alone"*.
We will sway together under the sparkling dew of the willow.

Do you feel it?

The earth has slowed her spinning in anticipation of your return.

*Worship etymology: To step boldly into our original condition of worth.

*I've spent most of my life searching for "home". The participants in this class helped me
to realize that I am home when I fully express myself and my experience. They gave me
the courage to want to speak my truth and caught me when I jumped. My poetry can be
found on Instagram @myhousebythecreek.*

The Wise Great-grandmother Oak
By Michelle Wells

Eulogy of a Wild Girl
By Clare Allen

There once was a girl full of spirit and light. She found joy in the universe, and in moving her body through the world. She ran, jumped and danced through life, exploring woodlands, hugging trees and making friends with wild creatures.

One day, driving through the Vale of Glen Rhinnes with her family, her father slammed on the brakes of the car, barely missing a deer bounding across the remote road in front of them. The young stag bounced across the grass into a meadow of wildflowers, then stopped to stare back at them, brazen in his innocence.

The girl did not hesitate. She climbed out of the car, and slowly scrambled across the ditch on the side of the road. As she crossed the meadow, she held out her hand, angled gently in front of her in invitation. Her eyes were fixed on those of the deer, who stood, quivering, watching her in return. She murmured quietly to him, noting his ears flagging, and his soft, wet-leather nose twitching at her scent. Her parents stood, anxious and awestruck, but she knew she was meant to be there, in this moment with this creature fixed between grass and sky.

Suddenly he startled a little and turned his haunches, facing three-quarters away from the girl, but with his left eye still fixed on her. She paused, letting him settle, now no more than two arms' lengths away. She slowed her breathing, and relaxed, feeling the pleasure of the movement, and saw his muscles relax, too.

And then, she stepped forward and touched his thigh. Just a brief tactile glimpse of fur, as he awoke from his trance, and bounded away into the tree-line at the edge of the meadow. She stood for a moment, holding her hand up where a moment before he had stood, and the enchantment broke as she heard her parents come crashing towards her.

The story became a family legend. "She has a way with animals," her parents told everyone. It puzzled her. She had just tuned in to the frequency of the universe for a moment. She had felt the energy of the beautiful creature with the soft eyes and velvet muzzle, and reached out to it.

But a gift can be twisted and hammered into vocation in the forge of education. She pursued that connection to animals academically by becoming a vet. I basked in the pride of her parents and teachers, and mistook it for love. I killed the girl with the spirit of a wood sprite and the heart of a Valkyrie, and bargained away her life for the paltry reward of approval.

And yet…there is still beauty in the sunlight, dappling through the late-summer leaves, in the warmth of a dog, pressing his body against my legs at the end of the day. When I notice these things, I remember her, that wild girl with the heart of a Valkyrie.

I am a global nomad currently living in Cambridge, England. The mother of two extraordinary boys and wife of a third, I have worked as an equine vet, completed a PhD in education and now teach vet students. I have always tinkered with writing, but never allowed myself to take it seriously, until now...

Uncle Karyk's Cottage
By Jindra Cekan

Uncle Karyk's one-room summerhouse in the Czech countryside was a wooden structure that he had built from leftover garage planks. It was with mischievous pride that he told us he'd stealthily "repurposed" the garage that used to sit behind the family's mansion. It took weeks for him and some pals to move the planks, but he figured the mansion's new communist owners were too busy living the high life in it to notice its garage slowly disappearing. He rebuilt it several streets over on a narrow bit of family land that had so little value that it hadn't been confiscated. No one important noticed either, he said, which indicated as much about his work as it did about the vacant judgment of their new rulers.

Like so many Eastern-bloc men, his greatest love was his "chata" (summer cottage). It was a motley crew who came there: my family's former wealthy friends who had lost all their property in the 1948 nationalization and became drivers or manual workers like my uncle Karyk, or doctors who still plied their trade, or those who never stopped working on farms – just suddenly were "collectivized," to former restaurant owners who had been demoted to being managers or waiters, and so many other nameless people who sat, merrily drinking in the yard with their mismatched table and chairs.

These gatherings would go well into the night, people telling stories, teasing one another about some nearly forgotten event from their shared youth-to-adulthood. When my father visited, he wistfully listened to the stories, because he had, after all, missed decades. My father brought to the table the gift of those missing years of the 1930s to 1940s, like one would bring a healing tonic; he resisted the discomfort of being left out of the spotlight and brought his fellow "Revnicaks" townies back to their youth.

One story came from the time they were fourteen, before he left for Swiss boarding school when a suit of armor crashed down the stairs of their great-grandparents' mansion, nudged by one of them when they crept up the stairs drunkenly in early morning. Another, at age ten, when their grandmother chased them out of the garden where they were chopping the heads off of cabbages in her servant-tended manicured garden. Why? They were vividly re-enacting a novel as Crusaders chopping the heads off of Moorish infidels with ceremonial swords taken from the dining room. For the listeners, no matter the economic rung, they laughed, for mischief is mischief.

Then my uncle and his visitors regaled us with funny 1950s to 1970s times: "Camping-in-Bulgaria-with-makeshift tents" stories or "when–our–first–car–

broke-down-and-there-were-no-spare-parts." These were stories from the decades my father couldn't return. Other people at the table piled their "do you remember" stories on top of his, a tower of words and emotions. As the evening progressed, my father and uncle sang old and new songs that made up for lost time, creating new stories together long past sunrise.

Jindra Cekan is a working single mom of two, a PhD in international development, a giraffe lover, a Czech-American and a fledgling writer, grateful to Martha Beck and her elves...

A Note From My Mom, And Maybe Yours
By Carrie Seid

Oh, my dear. Listen to me. Puh-leeeeeeze go ahead and give away my cashmere sweater sets. They are not divining rods to contact me, and they won't bring me back. And now that they've been dry cleaned, they don't even smell like Capri 120s mashed up with Revlon lipstick. Take them to Goodwill or make a quilt out of them. And for God's sake, get rid of those giant oxygen tanks! I don't need them to breathe. You're the one who needs to breathe, now, and choking your guest room with piles of my crap isn't helping you one bit.

I loved living in that little room, and wished I could have stayed there for the duration. I'll probably never forgive you for moving me out and into that horrid place, and though I pretend not to understand, I do. Throwing pillows and blankets and suitcases and crutches on the place where my bed used to be will not ease the pain of it. You won't forget, no matter how impressive your hoardy pile.

I do miss stuff, sure. I miss the thrill of opening those packages from QVC and showering you with glittering baubles made of Diamonique, purple tanzanite, and the greenest chrome diopside. I miss snow. And men. And cigarettes…oh how I miss cigarettes! And stargazer lilies.

But I'm right here, honey. We all are. If only you could see it, how we wrap ourselves around you like ectoplasm. We follow you kids around like stalkers. We're in your business, we're in your noses. We insinuate ourselves in your days, in your decisions, in your art, and in your food. We still constantly tell you what to do, question your career moves, snub our noses at your partners. We play in your hair like monkeys. We tease you with sightings in your dreams. You wear us around everywhere like an extra sweater you take in case it gets chilly in the movie theater. We are love at its essence, tiny pixies who slip into the tiniest of spaces, and bigger than anything you could ever touch.

So go ahead and clean that room out, sweetheart. It won't make a goddamned bit of difference.

We'll still be gone. And we'll still be right here.

Carrie Seid is a nationally recognized artist who also works as a high performance creativity coach. She also writes, conducts seminars, and speaks on the subject of creativity. Seid lives and maintains a studio in Tucson, Arizona. Check out her coaching practice on her website: www.carrieseid.com and her artwork on her other website: www.carrieseidart.com.

Midden
By Jessica Waite

Today, Jessica promised to confront *The Pile*. It had been shifting between the kitchen table and the hall closet for a long time. She'd told herself that she didn't have time, that she'd tackle it later, but she was lying. She avoided dealing with the pile, mainly because it might lead to opening *The Box*, a bigger, more terrifying secret she hid in the basement.

Jessica started on the fringe, non-paper items. A dog tag indicating a rabies vaccination in 2016…but which dog was it for? She couldn't remember. She felt like a failure and set down the tag. Was this how fuzzy-headed she'd become, how ineffectual? Could a tiny obstacle like this derail her? No, she called Panda over. He licked her chin as she examined his tags. "2016 rabies" was jingling with the others. Woodward leaned into the neck-scratch she gave him as she took off his collar to add the tag. Bolstered by puppy-love and this tiny victory, Jessica took on the pile.

Recycling: Drop-in gym class schedule. She shuddered, having attended not one of the many classes she'd highlighted in yellow. An unopened copy of *Wired* magazine. She'd been foisting those on Tyrone for months. Into the bin. Onward.

Filing: Sean had handled the bills, the service records for the van, all of it. Neatly and efficiently. She hated doing this stuff. Looking at a receipt from the physiotherapist made her back hurt. She wanted a break.

A few weeks ago, she'd bought a new tablecloth as a reward for sorting the pile. It might smell plastic-y, she now rationalized, taking the tablecloth outside to hang in the yard where the snow was newly gone and the sun was shining.

Coming back in, she noticed that the pile was much smaller. Tax stuff, yuck. Two sets of school photos: Grade 5 and Grade 4. She had only one child. These had been sitting, waiting to be cut into wallet-size and sent out. Too late now, she thought, and moved them to the filing cabinet.

A few minutes later, the table was bare. It occurred to her that with Easter coming up, she'd be seeing a lot of family. She retrieved the school photos and assigned the Grade 5 portraits to be distributed. She smiled, she was on a roll. She opened the Grade 4 envelope and held the two photos side by side to compare. Her young son's handsome face smiled at her in both pictures, but looking at them together made her gasp in pain.

The boy on the left had a father. The boy on the right did not. Could she see that transformation in his face?

This kind of question was the bedrock upon which piles were built.

Enough! She filed the older photos, no guilt. Then, she claimed her new tablecloth and spread it over the clear table. The cherry blossoms and songbirds cheered. She put the kettle on for tea.

Jessica Waite conserves love stories and fond memories at <u>www.endlesstories.love.</u>

ENOUGH
By Ceridwyn Mizera

I finally see the "gift" of Daddy dying first.

They were married 63 years. His love for her and us was never a question mark. Her love for him and us was a constant one.

Dad was luminous; Mom, shadow.

She didn't know how to be bright beside him.

Only after Dad's death, and for the time she survived him, did the true love Mom had for him and us shimmer to the surface, excavated by grace. No question remains.

It wasn't the same but it was enough.

Ceridwyn is a salty/sweet bookworm who can often be found meandering barefoot in nature, with a song on her lips, and sparkly pen in hand. Or in the kitchen baking a pie. She and her husband share their lives with two cats, with everyone living happily ever after. The End.

Gift Her With Eyes That Look Soft On Her Pain
By Carol Bonneville

To the woman reading this, whose heart has been torn through the loss of a baby. I see you, dearest one, this pain is almost too hard to bear. My heart longs, even to this day, to see the smiling faces of my two children who did not get to nestle into my arms, who never splashed with me through puddles. I miss them terribly as you will miss your child. I am here, I understand, I see you. xoxo

Today she will come
to the black cave of loss,
down the steep steps of grief
lies the bridge she must cross.

Past the creaky red gate,
rusted stiff by the rain,
past the shadows that whisper
their lies about blame.

Past dragons and witches,
past strange and known places,
past bridges now burned
to the rock with two faces.

And these guardians of hell
each a question will ask,
as she summons her truth
for this last awful task.

"Is that courage I see?"
"Is that fear I can smell?"
So she answers with "Yes"
in this cavern of hell.

Then onwards she'll pass
till she reaches this door,
and she'll pay with her tears,
as she paid once before.

And she'll whisper goodbye
to the jewel in her womb,
a treasure awaited
but taken too soon.

And her heart will break open
for the future that's passed,
for her dreams that lie shattered,
and hopes that are dashed.

And she'll turn to walk home
with a heart full of sorrow,
for what should have been
in her days of tomorrow.

Come Spirits of gentleness, Spirits of light,
Come Spirits of symmetry, that dwell in the night,
Come Spirits of healing, Come Spirits of prayer,
Come Spirits of mercy, and Spirits of care.

Feather her feet for the long road ahead,
Bandage her wounds in the places that bled,
Cloak her in softness, bathe her in love
as she rages and storms at the heavens above.

Stay with her, Spirits, till the storming shall cease,
gift her with calmness, acceptance and peace,
gift her with courage to live life again,
and gift her with eyes that look soft on her pain.

And one day she'll lift up her face to the skies
and smile at the life she can see with her eyes,
then she'll tenderly place two small seeds in the earth
for her children who slept through the day of their birth.

And she'll sing you a song with notes made of pain,
a lullaby formed from the sun and the rain,
a symphony played on the keyboard of earth,
that every new dawn is a day of rebirth.

You are the petals, but she is the rose,
You are the poetry, she is the prose,
You are the acorns, and she is the tree,
You are the droplets and she is the sea.

Carol is a quirky, feisty, passionate explorer of this thing called life. She is unapologetically herself. She has been a professional singer, an academic, and a cleaner. Originally from the UK with a fierce love of her Irish heritage, she now lives in beautiful New Zealand.

Rhinanthus minor
By Arwen Niles

I've taken to texting while driving. Letters to myself—peddling in half-truths, vying to be seen. The words squabble and rattle, but I don't mind. Some days are just like that. Truthless. Maybe gone to be born of another. Maybe waiting in the ether while we ready.

I text my way past the night market, autocorrecting, swerving. Past lean brown boys playing basketball in the shadows. Past the village mural. Past the spot where my husband and I last laughed together, running through the darkness, mile 5.

My giver-upper husband who doesn't know what he wants anymore. That sweet salve of a man who lent me lovebabies and made me—so very briefly—a mother. My sad soulmate who keeps trying to follow them out of this world.

He comes home and I am gone. Floors unswept, our now-separate beds unmade. Just in case another fleeting lovebaby would come to us in the night and try to break our hearts again.

We can no longer be trusted with our dreams.

In the trunk a kennel rattles from the coral roads. I've become a chariot of the unwanted: spending my days collecting garbage, and strays. The discarded evidence of possession.

My car smells of filth, and divinity.

...

My first baby liked to hike. My friends would shake the brown seedpods at my belly, God's tiny maracas. The blossoms like sweet peas, but gilded. An exquisite alien species. Little yellow rattle, maker of meadows, emblem of light.

We'd found a way to belong to this earth.

Back then we were still living the lies inside our warm bodies—those ripe, heavy fruits. Back when I was love manifest, two hearts beating within.

Back before the punishments began.

I will poison this body that betrayed us, my dear, each morning neatly offering up the empty bottles, glass prayers.

I will spend my days alone among the waste, thirsty, until I have earned the right to come back home.

My truths, like my babies, simply refuse to be born. A catastrophic anomaly, perhaps. Uninhabitable conditions. A vessel eventually empty. They were always their own becoming—or not—never ours to keep.

So I haunt the tides; they haunt me back. This time a faded rattle from someone else's baby, or maybe from the ocean depths—one of mine. I take it home, add it to my bounty, open a bottle.

Sometimes the suffering is sacred, and there just isn't anything left to say.

Arwen Niles is a trash-collecting treasure seeker who has, since writing this piece, put the final gestational touches on the child collectively referred to as Babylove. She lives on Guam and isn't as sad as she seems.

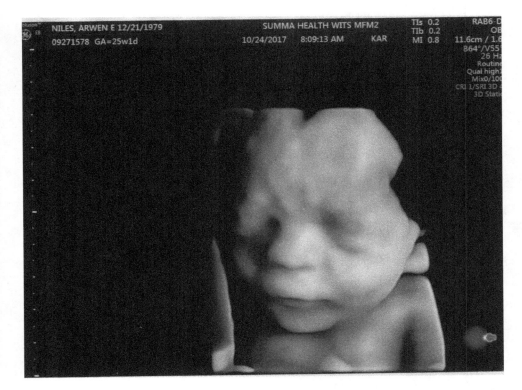

Babylove

Etheric Bands of Connectivity Through Time
By Judith Elaine Halek–Thriver

Vacuumed eyelids reflect prisms of distortion.
Where is the comfort? What is the truth?

Tears pour out like streams of neglected consciousness
Deeply embedded in forgotten memories.

Bathing in a pool of weeping widows tears,
Salty and healing are the paper cuts that sting.

Birthdays come and go and eventually never happen.
We are kept prisoners by clinging incessantly to celebrations of what is not.

Disregarded and placed in facilities,
We whittle away like a piece of rotting driftwood.

Voices echo through timeless chambers
Where minds are subdued by silent lullabies of unexpected treasures.

Books fall off shelves to reveal messages from mother's womb
Cradled in time past when dust is all that remains.

We seek this constant connection.
Where flesh has long time been mourned.

And when the veil is crossed,
The etheric bands of connectivity remain intact.

Waiting in quiet patience for density to still,
As receptors ignite, firing synapses compute capacities of interconnections.

Is the gap a figment of our imagination?

As we are the 'dreamer of the dream' in a non-existence time and space?

The old man, with scythe and hourglass, engages his trickery upon us.

He laughingly beckons us to distorted travels.

Are we against time, before time, behind time or for the time being?

Do we have no time? Is it happening at the same time or in one's own time?

The truth is: time flies, time is money, time and tide wait for no man.

We pass the time of day and in no time we come to understand, only time will tell.

For 35 years, Judith Elaine Halek has been the Director of Alternative Healing Modalities and Birth Balance. She's an accomplished international speaker, published writer and documentary filmmaker. In 1987, Judith assisted the first underwater birth in NYC and has attended over 1,000 births. She lives in NYC as a Cancer Thriver.

Eternal Return
By Bettina M. Stuetz

Dedicated to Sebastian Stuetz

As you enter into your darkness, know that you are not the first and not the last.
These are not harsh words to fear, they are words of eternal wisdom. This life
is created in circular spirals where birth and death are all perceived in divine
love. Our lives are all continuously unfolding, being created moment to moment.

In your darkest, blackest, most haunting time, therein lies the seed of love.
If you are willing to sit in the black abyss and allow this sadness to penetrate
every cell of your body, you will feel peace entering your heart where you no
longer thought your heart resided. This small seed of love and peace is the gift
I can offer you from my most dark night of the soul.

When you feel small and weak, hopeless and torn, this gift will be there for you.
Plant this seed in the center of your broken heart and water it with prayer. Stay
in the eternal now and just be with yourself and your pain. This gift I offer will
grow when you have faced every demon, every dark night, until you can face
them no longer, therein lies your sanctity.

Sit in hoop time, circular time and you will feel this seed growing and opening
and filling every void in your being. This is the seed of eternal love. It can never
die. It is the Eternal Return. The cyclical element of this universe. We sit in the
sacred circle of life and resonate through our hearts, each life connected
eternally to the other.

Be empty and still Heart
That I may hear the Wind
As it blows through the Forest,
Let me follow its path.

Be empty and still Heart
That I may know myself in the silence.
That I may know this Space.

Be empty and still Heart
That I may hear the voice in my breath,
That I may understand its teaching,
Let me follow its path.

Be empty and still Heart
That I may understand
That which is and that which is not,
That I may conceive of Duality.

Be empty and still Heart
That I may know Spirit,
Spirit that lies beyond perception,
Let me follow its path.

Be empty and still Heart
That I may dissolve,
That I may become manifest and un-manifest.
That I may become immortal.

My name is Bettina Maria Stuetz. I'm married to the love of my life. Our youngest son Sebastian Berthold Stuetz died at the early age of 6 years. He was vaccinated after birth with Polio and BCG. He reacted to the toxins in the vaccines. He suffered from either heart fibrillation or heart attack. The oxygen supply to his brain was decreased for an extended period. I nursed my son, who could not walk, not speak, not feed himself until it was time for him to pass on.

I have since his passing learned many alternative healing techniques including craniosacral therapy, shiatsu, yoga. My life revolves around healing the pain we all face. Finding the answers to all the questions. Becoming whole. Death has become my guru. In the Buddhist tradition this is what we should reflect on daily. We are here on this earth for a short time. Find your dharma and live your life how you intended. Blessings.

.

Love Will Sustain You
By Clare Smart

If I could step back in time to the day that my young husband was diagnosed with terminal brain cancer, what would I tell myself? What would I tell the ambitious, independent, achievement-focused, busy young woman who was trying to balance starting a family with career and settling into a new community? My younger self who knew as soon as she heard the diagnosis – that the structure of her life and all her dreams were no longer. What would I say as she ran her hand over her pregnant belly and cuddled her husband and 12 month old son?

I would say
                    Love will sustain you through the darkness.

Love will show up and support you.
In so many forms.
Open all of your doors and windows.
Welcome love in.
Make space for all the colours and shades of love.
The love of friends,
the love of strangers,
the love of your parents,
your love for each other,
the love of, and for, your children,
your love of the natural world and
the deep love within you for yourself.
It will teach you, surprise you and inspire you.
You will *all* be carried and connected by love.
And on the darkest, hardest days in the last few weeks on the cancer rollercoaster,
and then when you are navigating through grief,
some of your dearest friends will morph into guardian angels.
They will carry you and help you with exactly what you need.
Terminal cancer is a grey ominous cloud but throughout you and your young family will be showered by rainbows of love.
Grief will be a heavy swirling dark fog but you will find rainbows of joy whenever you look for them.
And when you emerge from the labyrinth of grief, you will find more laughter and love than you can imagine.

Love is the only reality. Let it in.

Clare Smart became a young widow and single mother to two children under five years of age when her husband died from brain cancer in 2012. Her blog, <u>https://rainbowsandrollercoasters.com</u>, *delves into the emotion-full experiences of cancer caring, grieving, solo parenting and dating again. She is a grateful yogi and every day finds colour, strength and joy by playing at the beach or simply admiring a flower.*

COMMUNION

I AM HERE
By Susan Telford

I know you cannot believe what has happened. You didn't deserve this.

Some people will tell you bad things happen to good people, that no one escapes the suffering. Others will tell you it is all an illusion, some Cosmic game designed to wake you up and enlighten you.

Right now, you feel that both perspectives are a crock of shit. Neither helps you in this moment, when the pain is so bad it affects your breathing, when you feel that you can't go on.

I'll be honest, I wanted to tell you that there is nothing wrong, that at some soul level, everything is unfolding as it must, that some part of you chose this. That is what I was going to say to you today, but the words stuck in my throat.

So, instead, I will hold your hand. I will make you tea. I will stroke your hair as you cry. I will listen to you as you tell me how life is for you right now. I will not make you wrong for feeling as you feel. I will not try to impose my view of reality onto what I cannot know to be true for you.

I will not leave you alone in your pain. I will not present myself to you as someone who knows anything better than you.

You are the authority on your own life. I am done with platitudes and promises of future bliss.

This is where life is happening, here amid the pain, the snot and the disappointments. The broken heart is real, the pain in the body hurts, the grief of losing what you love tears you in two. I will not minimise this with my stories of Fierce Grace and nothing wrong.

Can I just sit with you? Can I just love you exactly as you are?

That is all I have to offer you today.

I cannot fix anything for you, it is not mine to fix. All my words are meaningless now. Perhaps, in your own time, you will find your own words, your own path.

Perhaps, not.

How could I know?

Today, this is my path: to be with you as you face this unexpected horror that has left you bereft. The only thing I know for sure is that I will no longer reject this moment, no matter what is arising. I will not reject your experience or mine. I will not overlay this present reality with words of advice, no matter how well intentioned. I will not tell you how to feel, how to live, how to heal.

I looked into my heart today, for the wisest words I could give to you.

All I found was

"I am here".

This article was previously published in Thrive Global.

Susan was a Type A workaholic teacher who burned out. She recovered by unravelling her people pleasing tendencies and learning to listen to an inner voice. She calls this process "Slowing down to the speed of grace". Susan retrained as a life coach and now supports professional women to create lives that nourish, rather than deplete them. Connect with her via her website www.susantelford.com.

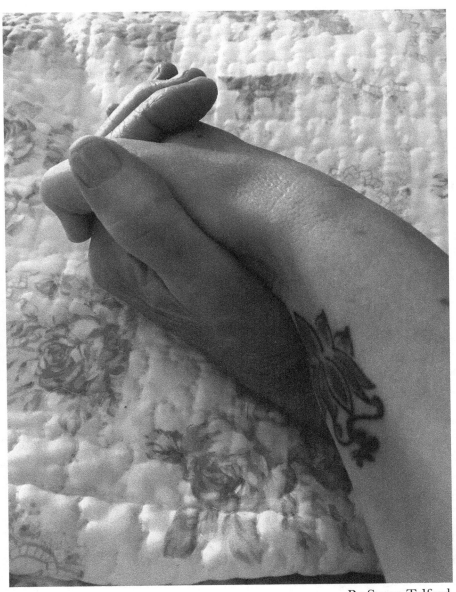

By Susan Telford

Vessels of Light
By Pamela Rae

We give away sunshine…

In mason jars galore.
With lightly placed lids —
Well-cared for, ventilated vessels:
Soul-rejuvenating words of light.
Offering warmth…
There's a jar
Unnamed,
For you.

We collect Sunshine…

We collect Sunshine…

For you.
Unnamed,
There's a jar
Offering warmth…
Soul-rejuvenating words of light.
Well-cared for, ventilated vessels:
With lightly placed lids —
In mason jars galore.

We give away sunshine…

Educating inner-city youth for over twenty-six years, Pamela's greatest joys include reading the beauty of her students' work, living in the moment, and loving her daughter. What it means to be a Vessel of Light is her first "mason jar message." Find her work on Instagram @mindfulmissclark.

if I could write a word
by mab

if i could write a word
a captured moment
a single emotion
a life time lesson
if i could write a word

if i could write a word
would it make a difference
a single understanding
an instantaneous connection
if i could write a word

were the printed letter heard
heard by those who read it
by all of those that need it
the affirming written word
were the printed letter heard

were the printed letter heard
heard in the place it comes from
to the space hidden deep inside some
thoses weighted defining words
were the printed letter heard

Margo Bothwell (mab), PreciousPresent@yahoo.com
Author, Artist, Brand Manager, Product development, with a focus on what's
important. Passionate gardener, lives and creates in Arlington, Virginia, with her
husband, a retired school teacher. Most days she can be found playing and creating with
her grands.

A Letter to My White People
By Hannah du Plessis

"I imagine one of the reasons people cling to their hates so stubbornly is because they sense, once hate is gone, they will be forced to deal with pain." – James Baldwin

I am sorry that it has taken me so long to write this letter, but here I am. My heart is worn through with hate. For a time my hate served me, suppressing the raw and roaring pain inside. It helped me distance myself from you.

But I was wrong. I have judged you harshly. I judged you as uncaring, yet I offered you no care. I judged you as narrow-minded, yet not a crumb of my curiosity reached you. I labeled you as blind, but I have never seen you. I accused you of silencing others, yet I have no ears for you. I judged that you hide in a self-protective cocoon, yet my hate shielded me from your presence. I condemned you as someone complicit in criminality, but I have never told you that I have transgressed myself. I despised the way in which you doubt and diminish others, yet I distrusted you and diminished you with my dislike. I blamed you for your addiction to power, yet I am no stranger to grabbing for control.

This hate is the cavity cleaving the red sea in half, leaving each of us an ocean unto ourselves. I have forgotten our shared foundation. I have forgotten that the currents can sweep us clean. This separation atrophies my belonging to life, to you, and to all the parts of me that are you.

But no more of that.

Will you consider taking a step towards trust?

I would like to practice being awkward together.
Is it too much to ask if we sit in silence?

I would like to listen.
Can we slow down so you can tell me what wears on you?

I would like to understand.
Might you show me glimpses of who you are becoming?

I would like to support.
Will you allow me to help you unfold into your next season?

I would like to let go. Our past is painful.
Could we stand together in the stream of forgiveness?

If you are not ready yet, please don't feel obliged. There is no rush. I'm not leaving. I'm practicing kindness.

A note to the reader: The author of this piece is white, and was born and raised in apartheid South Africa. As she came to understand the pain caused to people of color by well-meaning white folks who unconsciously uphold and enact oppressive behaviors, relationships, systems and structures, she became angry. She was angry at her white people for a long and hard season, but this anger disconnected her from them. This letter is a step towards reconciliation.

Hannah believes that the world our hearts long for is possible. As a facilitator and trainer, she helps groups learn processes and skills to become and create that world together. She is a glutton for the creative process. She loves frolicking with humans almost as much as solitude.

July Morning
By Cynthia Rome

So much can be forgiven on a July morning,
hose in hand,
looking out onto a meadow.

All inflated self-importance,
the rivalry of fellow women,
is rearranged
as I watch the invisible force of the breeze
play across the heads of daisies.

The foxglove stand tall, coloured in passion.
The brown grasses sing below them,
holding no malice.
The daisies bob their heads.

A competition for fertile ground,
the meadow its resolution.

There is no need for forgiveness in nature.

If I stepped out of my body,
I would surrender in full bloom.

Cynthia lives in the wilds of a small Gulf Island in British Columbia where she spends her time tracking the ways of the heart.

The Cedar and the Larch
By Sylke Laine

North Star Speaks
By Anastasia Brencick, MA, LMP

Between the inky black universe and the crisp white explosion of stars, an infinite number of possibilities begin. Grab them, any one of them, it doesn't really matter. Wherever you start is exactly right.

The gravitational pull will lead you home. It feels like a first kiss, or Christmas, or a dip in an icy lake after a hot day, or seeing a whale off to starboard, the grand body so quiet it cracks you open inside. This pull you are following is your destiny. Can you feel the vibrations in your spiderweb bones? But destiny is not pre-determined. Destiny shapes as you form words to articulate this longing. Your Stillness finds Itself emerging into words and, like rungs in a ladder, your next steps materialize. Follow this. It is just for you, a world created as you are creating. It leads you home. Don't fret, love, it will lead you home.

The isolation you made for yourself to feel safe is a lie. Break through the walls you are trapped behind. Reach your hand out to grab another's. Feel the power of wanting to be reached…in the strength of your own grip. It's okay to want help. Take this journey with loving hands at your back, holding your weight when you stumble, smoothing the worry lines from your face, massaging the tension from your shoulders. Ground yourself in the help of others, your oasis of rest. Receive their loving touch. We are never meant to travel alone for the entirety of our journey. That's the secret I can offer you. Write these helpers into your story. They don't know they are in your play. Cast them so they can find their gifts in being your ally.

You will inevitably come to places of disconnect. It is the way of it. It will feel dark and lonely. It is the natural way of things to come to this place, so call on your allies to meet you when you come out. You will come out of this, sweet one, don't worry. It only feels like you won't. Sometimes we swing so far away from our pull, we feel like we are lost, slipping from our place in an unknown constellation. You aren't lost. It is your aphelion. The blackness out in that part of the universe awaits its own storytelling. You will feel the gravitational pull again, reminding you that you were never ever separated from the perfect alignment that makes up the galaxies.

I love all things embodied. I write to understand the world we create and its meaning, while not concurrently self-digesting into primordial goo. I find life lessons to write about through hibernating, falling, failing, playing, learning and teaching. You can find more about me at <u>anastasiabrencick.com.</u>

Spirit Horse
By Jane Waugh

"Are you going to ride today?"

"Yes"

It sounded a firm yet breezy "Yes," but there was nothing breezy about it at all. There wasn't much that was firm about it either, teetering, as it was, on jelly legs and a faint heart. She was out of excuses, so sick of hearing them scrambling about, concocting their petty selves in her head, pushed to the tip of her tongue by the rising tide of fear and tumbling, unchecked, out of her mouth. Excuses that left her feeling deflated, dejected, weakened. Excuses that landed on deaf ears, everyone was so used to hearing them. It was decent of them to still ask the question; 'I'd have quit humouring me a long time ago,' she thought.

And stopped.

And turned.

The sweet, gracious mare with her perfect spirit horse markings, the medicine hat and shield, whose myth claims kept their warrior riders safe from harm, took a deep breath and sighed slowly: the sound of contentment. Millennia of wisdom shone from those beautiful, all-knowing, soulful eyes. The horse took a small step forward and touched her head to the girl's shoulder.

'*Please, get on, get on.*'

The girl felt the gentle, loving words ease into her consciousness. There was no sound. A moment passed and with it, a lifetime of doubt and worry. In that moment there was only a tender, boundless connection. Her hands tingled, her shoulders dropped and she, too, sighed.

"Ok, it's you and me sweetheart, we can do this," she whispered, reached her foot to the stirrup and swung into the saddle.

Vesper
By Colleen Raine

For a long time, I could only hear the long, rounded note of her wolf's howl clear and holy like a nun's prayer sung at midnight into the quiet, empty space. Her song slowly becoming my bedtime prayer to the moon and the night sky as I felt her soul leak through the cracks. My body moved with the surge of the inevitable uprising, tearing open the cage of what was jammed beneath our ribs.

And then she came to me as if my longing had dragged her away from some important business.

The sun had just set the first time I saw her: Standing in the damp gloom at the edge of the forest with its green painted ceiling bending over me, fireflies lighting up one by one like prayer candles in the shadowing alcoves at first night. I froze as I caught sight of the yellow glow of her unblinking eyes looking straight at me. Locked in her gaze, she slowly absorbed the measure of me. Lifting her chin to sniff the air that carried my scent as if one whiff was all it took.

What did she smell? What did she know of me?

An in-between kind of feeling pulsed to my extremities growing in intensity until my body closed in on itself. I shut my eyes and bowed my head. She left.

Instead of feeling relieved, I felt something else entirely. I felt deficient. As if during the time that I spent with her she had managed to carve a wolf-shaped space where I used to keep important things like my secrets. But now I was left with a vacancy that stood gathering dust and spider webs.

Every night, without fail, for as long as I can remember, my feet bring me back to this same spot and I wait for Wolf. I don't have to wait long because she always comes to me. She comes to the tree line, but never in the exact same spot. Standing half-hidden behind the pillars of the trees and curtaining leaves, teaching me to look for her. I feel her, before I see her, in cold fingers that touch my back and crawl up my spine landing with a touch between my shoulder blades tingling in ripples up my neck and around my jawline. My sweaty palms grip my shirt and then the base of my neck as if my crossed arms and hands could shield my heart and barricade my jugular. At the very least she could end it all with one well-placed tooth, rip me open and expose with surgical precision what makes me tick.

While my neurons furiously grip with their hardworking little tendrils and my brain tries another vainglorious attempt to unravel this mystery by efficiently stuffing this experience into a well-defined box, she stands still and holds me in her gaze until we both know we have been seen.

I am a creator; I carry the chaos of creation, bouncing from one convolution to another. As the main support crew of people who are dyslexic, we endured an excruciating struggle to get to the launch-pad-stage. It shaped me. It left its mark on my skin. In those darkest hours, light writers literally saved my life. It's time to pay it forward.

Red Deer with Pink Mandala
By Marion Perepolkin
Acrylic on canvas
https://society6.com/marionperepolkin
yourartyourway@gmail.com

Rooted by Love
By Jenny Lee Rowe

Traipsing through the forest, the reindeer yearned to rub her tiny antlers against a tree and pretend to be a buck, or, better yet, a stag ramming twelve-tined antlers. Bucks use antlers to fight, and those winning bucks had always ignored her, so today she trod far from the calving site. She spotted a magnificent tree with the kind of bark that holds rivers of sap. She tested her antlers against the thick tree skin, recalling the bucks laughing as their tilted heads bounced off the tree. She began butting, and though pain shot into her head and behind her eyes, she told herself she was stronger than her sister deer with their fat bellies and pitiful antler nubs. She struck harder and her hoof slipped, landing her small antlers in the join of two low branches. Panicked, she tugged, and fear spiked in her chest as the tree gripped.

Would it be a bear or a coyote?

She shivered.

Her tears gathered on the thick tree roots like prisms spinning sadness. Motherless, she had been nursed by a surrogate doe. She sobbed harder and then froze at the sound of a rustle.

A wily fox to bite my neck?

She shuddered and yanked.

"Who, who," sang an owl.

She held her breath.

"Are you wishing to die?" the owl piped.

"Am I what?"

"You have been weeping and imagining all sorts of terror."

"Well, I am stuck. Do you see my plight?"

The owl was silent.

"Hey, wait. You know what I am imagining?"

She heard a soft hum from the owl's breast, and she yearned to straighten her head. When stags of legend accept an arrow to the chest, they grant life force to the hunter who honors death by gazing into departing eyes.

"Why don't you gaze into the eyes of yourself as a fawn?" the owl crooned.

She pictured her motherless brown eyes full of fear.

"Go on," the owl nudged.

Her mind's eye gazed into her bewildered fawn eyes, and a bright feeling softened her chest. Just then the sun poked out, and light through the leaves dappled the earth, casting a shadow mirror of her antlers between the branches. She saw that if she tilted her head just so, she might free herself. She pulled and some of the thick bark crumbled. She straightened her stiff neck toward the owl, but it was gone.

The giant tree roots bulged under her hooves like thick antlers in the soil. Hoof to root, she soared through the forest all the way to the calving site, where weary new mothers cherished her tender gaze.

Grateful to my classmates for showing up—I have learned so much from you. And the best part? All of the acceptance and freedom to explore and play words together in this dream of life.

Wild Creature
By Fatima Viola

I love you. Lost, hurting, sitting at the bottom of a well, afraid that you will never see the light, that you will rot, alone, and all the gifts you doubt you have will rot with you.

But you are not alone, I am here, and so are the others of our tribe. Can you hear us singing to you?

I know the world makes no sense—it hurts like jagged edges of bone grinding against each other, and you feel too tender, too soft to ever belong. Shame and ugliness cling like a second skin, but oh my dear, you are so, so beautiful. Your eyes are too filled with tears to see your own light.

I see you. You are loved. You belong. There is magic in the world and you will find it. Yes, soon.

The pieces of bravery you cut off and cast away in order to fit in are waiting for you. It is the small self that cowers in the dark, desperately trying to hold up the walls as the earth shakes and dust falls from the ceiling. This is the cracking open.

My darling, this darkness is the struggle of birth. Something wondrous and lovely is being born. I know it's hard, but don't be afraid of the wild creature trapped beneath your skin. It is your true self.

Your truth, your strangeness, is welcome in our forest. The trees told me they love you, as I do. Rest—you are finally home.

Fatima Viola is a poet, a dreamer and a tree shaman. She can be found in the forest with flowers and twigs in her hair listening to the trees singing.

Homecoming
By Tracy Cottrell

I stand on the crest of the hill
Waiting. Open. Empty. Almost myself.
I hear her,
The tired scrape of weary feet,
The muffled rumble of loosened rocks signaling her approach.
The weight of her burdens, her sorrows,
Her arid pain, birthed from perceived lack,
Shouting silently, pushing air aside,
Making way.

Her inevitable pause
Quiet, softening, heavy,
Whisper her struggle to lend her nerves
To the haunting refrain of Onward.
Don't stop. Can't stop.
Allow breath, hear heart, and follow hope.

I take a step towards her
And reach out my hand,
She does not look up
Until a tightly held sob escapes
And she gasps for air.
Even still, her head comes up slowly
Her eyes are ancient
Reddened from tears that started
In the earth, rising through feet, legs, belly
Rushing through heart and throat,
Until they are swimming,
Through eyes and onto cheeks.

Past the watery blur, she sees me.
"Is it you?" she sobs, and her words strike my heart like tiny hammers.
Now her tears rise up through my heart, my throat, my eyes,
I welcome them.
Cleansing streams of release, gratitude, restoration, rebirth.

The heavy, rough cloak of what she was falls from her shoulders
Landing in a heap behind her.
She stands taller, straighter, who she is now rising,
Her hands touch her face.

She feels the mask of Ugly and Shame and becomes still.
Her fingers softly probe until she finds the edges
Then gently, so gently
Peels the dead skin away.

She takes off the worn, dirty sweater of violation
And tosses it down the hill, turns to share a smile of triumph.
Her radiance spreads from head to ground,
She glows.
She is not young or old, she is ageless beauty.

I open my arms and she comes to me.
We hold each other just tight enough
To feel our edges begin to blend,
Her heart beats with mine
She is the marrow of my bones
Her unrelenting strength, my strength.
Her knowing. My wisdom.
Me. Her. Us.
Now. Here. Together.
Ourselves. Myself at last.

The air shifts.
A soft whisper of welcome.
The sky, the earth, the trees
All breathe into us,
With us, for us, and us for them.
One. Whole. Now. Love.

IMMANENCE

Once in a Lifetime, Same as it Ever Was
By Judith Stewart

So many journeys.
Is it perfectionism, impossibly high standards or continued failure to learn
That has me take so many?

My sense is that I know the ticket was punched,
Most likely chosen by me,
In the Dreaming.

Arrivals into the new, nervous and curious, overwhelmed
By different slices of the world
Again and again.

Departures that are solitary sadnesses.
The searing pain of loss, as my world shifts and I lose intimacy.
My little light, so temporary, moves again …
And that life goes on without me—
How so? And what will it mean to rhythm
When I turn up, like a ripple, in the next place?

Both union and isolation are tied up in
A glittering string of short stories.
Familiar lessons.
A procession of tiny births and deaths,
Resplendent like the Magi.

The glorious secret is to know
That I have left myself clues of reassurance
Everywhere.
Across time and place, and
If I keep my heart open
The teachers will appear, the 'crazy chances' will be steadfast
And my path will open before me.

In this land, now,
The ancestors are in the country, embedded
In the landscape, with their stories
Of living, the sense of it or its non-sense. Present, honoured,
As our knowing is in our hearts. Deeply felt.
We have the responsibility of custody and compassion
For them and their stories, for ourselves, for trust.

This time round, Mouse, you will try and understand that
Leaving is not leaving when your heart comes too, and the glorious loss of self
Which comes in the new and vast, as much as when you find wild synchronicity,
Is communion.

No need to show up large and loud,
You are already here.

*Judith is on a seemingly endless tour of the world that brings both joy in new
experiences and sadness in departures. Every move she makes ... ! ... breaks her open
and reminds her of her vulnerability and how she is connected to the everywhere.
Magic! xx*

Already There
By Johanne Lila Larsen

The night falls fast and early now. There's a bite to the air, it has winter in its saliva.

The fuzzy outline of my naked body shimmers up to me through the night-blue surface of the water. The color of flesh falling into the disappearing of day.

I'm growing out hair in all kinds of places that have been pruned and contained and shamed and made ready for display, like quivering puddings. I just don't care anymore. It's my hair. It's just hair. Should anyone care, I couldn't care less. I see it through the surface, like seaweed.

My feet are disappearing in the end closest to the house, where the light from the windows are blocked. The reflection of warm light in the windows swims softly on the canvas of water around my knees.

The night is almost silent. I can hear a woman's voice. It's shrill. Other than that not even the trees make sound.

The color of the fir trees is different in the light from the orange flash light, standing upright on the edge of the wooden porch. The porch is makeshift like everything else here. The trees an almost unreal, superficial green, tinged with blue.

There, in the old cedar wood chips, that have now lost their scent, the snake escaped right before I stepped on it the other day. I felt its fear, before I felt my own.

The burnt-dry needles fall from the sky, silent as the early-autumn version of snow.

I thought 'shivering with delight' was a thing made up by people selling romance novels. But my body does it—shivers. Like it's cold, even while fully submerged in the dark, warm water.

In the moment I know: This is it. A silent night. Towering trees. A house so tiny, it has neither bath, nor kitchen. But a warm bed. Do we really need more?

The ocean so close that I return at day's end with pockets lined with sand and heavy stones that speak.

And a tub full of nighttime water, which I can stretch my aching, naked, aging body into and feel comfort. Even just for this one moment.

Now: I live my yearning, I'm already there. This second.

It's all we ever had anyway. All that ever mattered is always already there.

Johanne Lila Larsen is a journalist, photographer and unapologetic mystic. After having completed the entirety of the Camino de Santiago on her own, she returned to her native lands to find she had become a stranger. She sold all she had, and went out in the world, a perpetual pilgrim.

Finding Our Voices
By Katrina Allen

It is waiting.
That space we could inhabit
if we tried to sing like wolves or ride the comet of a bear.

We must wrench our hearts open,
let our lonely calls ring out.
Softly at first, barely there,
but rising.
A flood of voices to chill the bones with awe.

All of us learning and loving and leaning forward into strong winds.
Which may be fierce and blow against us,
but by doing so
they show us home, and hope, and friends.

I promise that in time
the bleakness and the winds will fade —
mere shreds with ragged edges adrift in crystal skies.

And then behold —
we will be standing as our own tall selves,
laughing and strong,
wreathed by love
and the reverberating echoes of our hearts.

For now, look deep and trust your truth.
We need not take grand journeys
or report the words of queens.
Quiet voices murmur
of hope beyond our fears.

In the world, light is waiting.
Look, outside the window
where small birds rustle about the business of living.
We can go and sit beside them.
Savoring the moment,
and our place in it.
Scraping emeralds out of ordinary days.
Sipping in wonder,
with our sleeves rolled up.

Katrina Allen is a Vermont artist who creates colorful nature-inspired impressionist paintings. At <u>katrinaallenart.com</u> she blogs about painting, creativity, and life lessons learned from art. She loves blue paint, fluffy peonies, chocolate chip cookies, and looking out the window at the birds and wild creatures who visit her yard.

The Secret of Stars
By Wendy Wyatt

To delight in dreaming dogs
Or swaying on a broomstick trapeze
The weightless wonder of trampolines

All gave flight to childhood wonder
Contemplating the composition of sky
While tracing clouds and contrails

Surrender to stillness as it delights
In dandelions and dreams of circuses
Behold my fear of dragonflies now transcended

Finding galaxies in grasshoppers and endless green
I discovered the invisible could be seen and felt
When calibrating cognitive dissonance

To my sisters in atomic connection,
Give me courage to free my sight
From ancient myths and golden dragons

Hold me in the cobwebs of bliss
Oblivious to the piercing death
While spun stories tether me to the map

Of wild transformation
In the celestial slumber of survival
In feeding another's needs, do we find what we desire?

With curiosity as my compass
And instinctual rhythms as my guide
My heartbeat finds the fractal echo of the universe

Loosening intellect's rein on sight,
Cadenced articulations dispatched,
Longing to be lost to indigo nights.

For then will I know the secret of stars?

Wendy Wyatt is a dreamer, a seeker and aspiring writer. She lives in the urban sprawl of Los Angeles, but longs to live in a cabin in the forest, where she can practice her crafts, and invite others to come remember how to commune and be with nature. You can find her at gypsyheartww@gmail.com.

By Wendy Wyatt

Perfection
By Linda Amato

You wait for me to acknowledge you daily,
To glance out beyond the walls of this home that sits upon your magnificence.
Sometimes I do, other times I get too busy.
It seems the hustle and bustle of life take me away from the beauty of your sight.
Today, the glowing stream of your water made my heart skip a beat.

Your vastness, calmness, and serenity allow me to be nurtured by your essence.
Even when you are angry, I know you are naturally cleansing yourself of debris.
It saddens my soul to see your sorrow,
All that you endure for many,
For the clueless here!
Today, I feel blessed because of you.

When I created you, it was for sustenance, love, light, and beauty.
A home for all!
Still, some have come to trash you, to violate you, but mostly to disregard your purpose.
It is you that gives us life.
Perfection could be your title.
However, we call you Mother.
It is your Nature to take it all in stride as we abuse you continuously.
Today, I am honored to live with you.

I cringe to think what life would become without you.
I worship you for many things but mostly for the gifts that you offer up.
Your foundation, the earth, connects us as one.
The waters that flow give us a choice to also go with the flow of life.
The fire that warms us from the sky beckons to us to become aware.
The air you offer allows us to breathe daily to exist.
Today, I cherish that I am witness to you.

Your beauty is beyond the land, trees, waters, birds, fish, animals, plants, sun,
stars, and moon, which blanket us with all that we would ever need.
You are the only universe that many refuse to see.
I am in awe of your belief in us that we can change, that we can respect all that
you are in this life experience we share.
Today, I say thank you...

As a woman, wife, mother, and grandmother, I write and I write and I write! My entire
life has been about writing! God had a laugh at this and after raising four children, I
became a Reiki Master, Metaphysical Practitioner, Self-Published Author, Energy Healer,
and Blogger.

Nature's Symphony
By E.L. (Betsy) Kudlinski

"Don't resist, Lynx, you are doing nothing wrong. Accept what *is*, and sense the beauty."

This was not the first time she'd heard this. It was Hummingbird, the dragon shaman's, mantra: *everything is right, it will come in time, don't get frustrated.* She didn't understand what her teacher meant, but she was drawn to the peace and love that emanated from her every feather. Hummingbird was always patient with her. As if she was standing outside of the conversation.

"Close your eyes, fledgling. What do you hear?"

So she tried again. She stood, feet apart, arms by her sides, eyes closed, breathing quietly, and listened.

Silence.

Except... It *wasn't* silent.

"I hear my beads and bells. The wind through the pines. Your feathers as you move."

Hummingbird started singing quietly.

At first, all Lynx could hear was the inhuman voice: several octaves in range, fluting trills and clicks and (almost) bellows.

Then, as time passed and she relaxed into listening, she began to hear more.

The song seemed to weave into and out of the sounds around them. The breeze was blowing through the trees, *whooshing* and tapping branches together. There were small birds singing, too, in counterpoint to the dragon song. As Lynx adjusted her position, her own shuffle seemed in rhythm with the song.

It couldn't be on purpose, yet somehow, all of the noises had worked their way into the song.

But it was more than just the sounds. There was a floral scent on the air. The pond near them was at its late summer level, and the damp smell of mud and rotting vegetation harmonized below the sweet notes.

The breeze came again and blew her hair around her face, and instead of irritation at the strands and beads against her mouth, she felt it as part of the whole.

Lynx opened her eyes. At first she watched the dragon, occasionally flicking her wings, a descant to the song. Then she noticed other movement, the birds and a few small animals rustling the pond grasses, the wind bending tree branches.

Then she saw the *colors*, and the contrast of light and shadow. Somehow, *everything* was coming together to create a full sensory symphony. Lynx basked in the harmony of it.

When Hummingbird stopped singing, Lynx drew in a breath to protest. But her teacher pinned her with a look. She understood that she was to stay quiet, keep listening. The lesson wasn't over.

And it wasn't. She heard the music continue. It wasn't the dragon's song, but instead, the song of the woods. Lynx realized that nothing had been creating music *with* Hummingbird. Instead, she had been singing with an ongoing orchestra. Any dissonance was punctuation to the whole. Even *she* was part of the whole, from the chiming bells in her hair to the scent of sweat from her day's exertions. She only added to the richness of it all.

And she understood, it was incredibly beautiful, peaceful, *right*.

A nature/animal/book nut looking forward to a fabulous life as a ...? Perhaps I'll start as a best-selling Fantasy author!

Feather
By Mary Walker

feather

how you keep a bird aloft, I do not know

part of a bird, part-bird yourself

bird, part-sky

sky, part-earth

earth, part-space

space, part-time

time, all that ever was

all that is

time

space

earth

sky

bird

feather.

writer, mother, homeschooler

Crayon
By Barbara Barnett

The mirror reflects smoky-gray
particles, life itself.

No Thing, Every Thing.

Spin, swirl, change.

Create imagination, carefree
openness, flashing golden sparks.

Hearts form a precious, waxy,
yellow Crayola Crayon.

I am living in western North Carolina in a tiny house community. I am launching a three-part program, Stop Stopping Yourself. Part I is aerobic exercise, Leslie Sansone's Walk 15 Live. Part II is Dr. Madan Kataria's Laughter Yoga. Part III is in-person Martha Beck's Wayfinder Coaching basics. Fun is a primary goal for my life.

A Book's Tale
By Seja Ateia

<u>Foreword</u>

Oh, cherished book,
You are holy love
and loved wholly.
You are a sanctuary,
a portal to other worlds.
You provide salvation
as a teacher,
a lover,
a friend.
On occasion,
you may serve
as a door stopper
or the unsung hero
to a table's wobbly leg.
But bless you,
you show up,
purpose unquestioned,
always ready to serve.

*

You enter the world,
pristine,
unsullied,
your lustrous glow,
enticing.
The mere touch
of your smooth skin
sends a shiver
down your spine.
Your story is
a mystery still,
waiting to be discovered.
As you open,
your spine cracks—
marrow splayed bare,
secrets undressed.
Your guts on the page,

reveal gems
in spaces between.
Inked across your chest:
the pencil of God.

The time has come.
Fireworks.
Story ends.
Truth begins.

*

Epilogue

Your pages,
wrinkled,
your words,
faded,
your smell,
musty.
You have come
unbound,
as a most beloved book
should be.

Seja Ateia is a Life coach, a wayfinder and a wild dreamer. She loves to write, travel and cook but her biggest passion is helping people find their magic and live their best lives.

Dog Hair Stories
By Anne Woods

In the beginning, you see dog hair as evidence: you need to clean the house better, and more often. Evidence to prove you are a rumpled adolescent to everyone else's adult. Other people have clean floors, you think. Other people have crisp, tailored wardrobes entirely unsullied by dog hair.

You misunderstand the message, so I repeat it, shedding downy Post-its on every surface. On your floor, on your most adult clothing, on your pillow. I laugh and tuck a few stray hairs in your mouth.

Look again, and see: that he barreled in from the sunshine, smiling, trailing dry leaves and dirt. That he slept on this rug for happy hours, then fishtailed on the rough surface, pinwheeling his legs in the air, woofing in pleasure.

Sweep the kitchen floor and gather memories of all the nights you two laughed together over a bottle of wine, teaching him to sit, to eat from a fork, to delicately slurp one long strand of pasta offered from on high.

Brush off your jeans and feel how he squares his big body across your thighs, leaning in, stepping on your foot for good measure. How you bend down to hug him, every time, swooning when his coat smells of petrichor.

——

On a trip to New York, pull a single white strand from your sleeve and hold the weight of how much you miss him. Tell yourself that someday, the dog hair in your hand will be all you have left of him. Feel the thought crush your heart in your chest, feel grief sparking like static down your arms.

Dare to trust what this body tells you: it is a lie.

Tentatively, gently, turn your story inside-out and try it back on: This dog's soul and your own—like his double coat and your favorite sweater—are forever entangled.

Smile then, and weave the coarse white hair back into the fabric.

——

A Great Pyrenees sheds hair the way a heart pumps blood or a mind creates thoughts: all day, every day, all his life. Brushing becomes your ritual. His breath, your meditation bell. Bring yourself to the floor. Pull the brush down his back with one hand and stroke his coat with the other, over and over, drawing a rhythm. Dissolve knots where you find them. Marvel at his lion's mane. Laugh and stretch when he's had enough and runs away from you. Bow low as you make a downy offering to the compost pile and the birds.

In the end, there is simply this: your hands scratching his shoulders, feeling the soft sable of his ears. No story. No past. No future. All of Creation gazing out in adoration, first through brown eyes, then through green. His big shaggy head pushing into your chest as your heart and your life expand. As the dog hair drifts in the breeze, becoming Love.

Anne Woods is a writer, artist, and fledgling farmer. She and her family live in Austin, Texas, under a light dusting of dog hair.

Praise Song for the Gubudubu*
By Kashi Rainbow Starlight of the Golden Heart
as told by her Mama, Melanie Phoenix

*Pronunciation: (gŏo -BOO-də-boō)

I watch and listen as Kashi and her twin brother, Magic, play. Kashi is unusually verbal for a dog but one must listen carefully. One day as she burst fireworks of joy around the room, I heard her murmur, "Gubudubu."

Not out loud. Dogs' mouths can't form complex words. Magic clearly enunciates, "Oh Mama," or when asked to name our very best president ever, he replies, "Obama!" without hesitation, but "Gubudubu" would be a bit much for any dog. Kashi speaks so that I hear her inside myself. With the word "Gubudubu" appeared a picture of a toy and the sensation of carrying it in her mouth.

"Kashi!" I exclaimed, "Is this Gubudubu?" I touched her bright green, squeaky alligator. Delighted that I understood, joy fireworks burst like a Fourth of July finale! Henceforth, we addressed that toy as Gubudubu.

A week or so later, I heard "Gubudubu" when Kashi had a different toy. I stopped and listened.

"Kashi," I asked, "is that Gubudubu too?"

She continued playing, but I noticed her voice move into my knowing like a sunrise slowly filling the sky. She said, "This thing that causes me to feel joy."

Oh! I understood! Gubudubu is a bringer of joy! A piece of stick, a fragment of toy, a muddy tennis ball, anything Magic has, Mama's smelly sock (oooh oooh, Gubudubu, Gubudubu!).

I told Kashi, "You are my Gubudubu." She swooned backward into my lap. Magic nosed his way under my hand. "You too, Magic. Bodhi and Sparky and Mama Terry too." Sloppy puppy kisses filled the room with giggles.

Eager to learn the way of unconditional joy embodied by these fur-suited beings, I requested a paean to Gubudubu. Kashi sang me this song.

> Oh, my precious Gubudubu,
> I hum zikr to you, hmm, hmm,
> as I dance quick-footed round and round and
> laugh with Rumi and Hafiz.

Kashi
By Melanie Phoenix

Oh, benevolent joy thing
of starlight and hummingbird hum
and soft fluffy something oh so lovely to pull out,
I hold you in my mouth and
together we chant *Love Love Love*
into all things everywhere and everywhen.

Hmm, hmm, hmm,
I wiggle every me-part,
dance and giggle and now is joy and
happiest of sweetest luminous days is now is joy!
Love is joy is dance is sing is now
is you, oh Gubudubu.

Hmm.
Hmm.
Hmm.
{Laugh}

Melanie Phoenix loves magic, language, and dogs. When all three come together as they did in this true story, that's her greatest gubudubu. Melanie lives in Santa Rosa, California, with her adorable wife, Golden Retrievers, and cat. She and Kashi are collaborating on writing a memoir.

TRANSCENDENCE

Come Out and Play, Spirit
By Mer Boel

"Come out and play, Spirit!"

I laugh, hearing my dolphin friend's heart-message, along with the quiet rushing of oceanic gel vibration. My Expediter work is waiting for me. It's the beginning of my shift.

"Thanks Soul, I'm with you always," I send back, along with an image of my hair streaming in the wind. Of course, he has no hair to speak of! My friend teases me back with an image of him moving smoothly underwater, something I yearn to be able to do.

"Can we play together, later?" Soul asks.

"That's a Big Yes" I send back. "And we can play now too while we're serving…"

"I'm on Water Tuner duty today, Spirit," he reminds me, and I breathe in his mastery of water to boost my strength for the day ahead.

I take in the Main Crystal Display mounted on the back wall. (Yes, we're old-school here at LightTuners ESP; we use external visuals to augment the more usual in-line delivery.) I see that there's one last-minute addition to the schedule: our Iron-Tuner is on her way to Buffalo, in the northern part of New York State, to protect and soothe some steelworkers engaged in high-rise construction. Expediter Soleris is standing directly in front of the display. He sends a quick-hearted "Hello Emera" and I see an image of the swirling, dark dust storm that indicates the increasing panic of the steelworkers. Soleris finishes up expediting several situations around our territory, wanting to see Level 3 Calm or higher everywhere before he signs off.

I open my internal web sensor to view the change-over activity of our tuners—as some continue their shift, some sign out and others sign in—and see that the high quality of the tapestry of soul threads connecting all major hub points around the globe is being maintained well in our territory. The colors are vibrant, threads feel strong, and the associated crystal energies are properly engaged. I love this part of my play as Expediter!

Pring! Ah, a quiet hand-bell chime—my first call is coming in! Quickly I put on my headset, because I can tell this is from our Meeting-Tuner, as her powerful energy thread is lighting up the United Nations in NYC. And Moira prefers to actually speak out loud when she gets in touch. Did I mention we were old-school?

"Hi dear! What's up? How're the meetings going?"

"I need a PowerUp for ten remote LightWorkers to tune into the UN president. He is feeling discouraged and desperately needs retooling rejuvenation, but my local group is overcommitted right now."

"Sure, the altimeter is still on the PowerUp setting." I reach internally for the switch and toggle it to ON, adding the parameters she requested. "Thanks for staying on top of it, Moira!" I enjoy the pearly glow crocuses she sends, and I send back the local creek burbling with melted snow run off. (It is springtime in most of our physical territory.)

To Be Continued...

Mer is a composer of music, a Highly Sensitive Person and empath who also writes, takes nature photos with her iPhone, and sends healing into the world as best she can.

The Everythingy
By Alise James

Dear God, Krishna, The Universe, Spirit, Allah, Light, The All-Knowing-Nothingness-Everythingy,

I want to split up.
I've thought about this long and hard, and I need you to know it's over.
It's not that I don't love you and I don't want to be with you. I do.
But you just attract too many jerks.
It's not your fault. You've got a lot to offer.
But here's the thing—it's exhausting keeping up with you. I already feel like I'm punching above my weight and then there's the endless pressure that everyone puts on you when you hang around your place. It just smells of smug.
It doesn't matter what name you're using or if you use the back door or the window, you're always surrounded by users and wannabes and rule-makers and hypocrites.
Even though we hooked up once and it was amazing, I just don't wanna put myself through all that shit again just for another little taste.
I'm sure you think it's pretty lame, me writing to you and not telling you myself after everything we've been through, but I know if you're around I'll just change my mind, so I'm writing you this letter. It's the only way I can be strong.
Don't be all merciful and loving and come meet me where I am. I know it won't last and at least I can be happy when I'm not aspiring for more.
I'm good with the way things are and I know you're peaceful regardless.
I'll always love you.

Alise. Xx

P.S. Thanks for always providing for me despite my lack of commitment. It's clear you are the bigger person.

Dear Alise,

You know me well enough to know that as content as I am, I can't be peaceful
without you. Your soul is like no other and I miss you.
It's not that I need you, you're right, I don't—but I do love you. With the kind
of love that you think you've tasted, but really, you don't have a clue.
It's big.
Perhaps that's what your afraid of. It's kind of all encompassing, but as
daunting as that sounds, you can still live with me and be loving to all. You can
still love your husband and your daughter. I know you are scared, but you can
actually love them more. I know how much because I sent them especially for
you.
I'm not writing to try and change your mind, you know its cheating nature. I'm
just really happy to hear your voice, whatever you have to say.
Try listening with you heart. You will find what you are looking for you. You
are flooded with love, but you have a little blockage in your receiving valve.
You are so right about the arseholes. There are many and they are all deserving
of our love. I can't judge them without judging you, and you know that judging
is the issue. Some peeps, you might like to forgive. Trust me, it will help.
The rules are laughable; they are the language of control and the opposite of
love.
Don't let them get in your way.
Rise above it. Give your soul some wiggle room.
I am in your every breath.
I can't live without you.

The Everythingy. Xx

A Letter From God
By Akumi Yokoyama

Dear Akumi,

I got your call. So great to hear from you.
I've been waiting to tell you some things. You seem ready now.

1) My name is God.
2) It's a common name around here.
3) The top 5 names in this realm, in your language, are: Muse, Angel, Spirit, Guide, and God.
4) I created Human Kind as a school project. I was praised and criticized for its complexity.
5) My sister created the Axolotl. So cute.

Photograph by Amanda Sofiarana

6) As my creation, I look after you to the best of my ability.
7) I am always cheering you on.
8) You are on Earth to experience being You on Earth.
9) You are allowed *and* encouraged to have fun with the experience!
10) Go see the Pyramids.

TTYL,
God

Akumi is slowly waking up to the fact that her world is more magical than ever imagined. She lives in Bellevue, WA, and daydreams about tropical beaches.

Please Stay Very Close
By Mary Geer

Please Stay Very Close,
Never release my hand.
Move me of your own volition,
Yet hear my Love's command.

Flow deeply into these lungs,
Beat strongly within this chest,
Infusing Grace and Guidance
Into every beat and breath.

Nourish the roots of my Belonging
And calm this worried mind.
Suffuse me with Joyful Laughter,
With Wisdom true and kind.

Stay close, I pray, when darkness falls
And even Closer Still,
When the path is lost, most treacherous,
When I feel it's all uphill.

Gently loosen these tight ties
To what I falsely label "Mine".
Bring Peace to this small Being.
Make this Life I live Divine.

Be the Strength that will inspire
And straighten up my spine;
The Courage that moves me forward
One turtle step at a time.

Reveal my Hardships' Blessings.
Relax resistance to the pain.
Teach me how to live this life,
Let me know it's not in vain.

Keep me Safely within your reach,
Please do not let me stray.
Show me I am Loved and Cherished
Every. Single. Day.

Mary Geer is a life coach who lives in the big, beautiful state of Montana. She loves the wide open spaces that are still wild and untamed. She strives to keep her heart, her hopes and her dreams as wide open, wild and untamed, too.

A Hospice Nurse / Novelist / Activist's Prayer
By Emunah Herzog

Dearest Beloved,

I lay before you my offering
My heart, my will, my life.

Please help me trust
That Your wisdom guides me
That Angels support me
And that I am where I'm supposed to be.

So that characters come alive on the page
And move, delight, and inspire many readers.
So that my patients live their last chapters
With as little suffering and as much meaning as they can.
So that I am a blessing to all who come my way
And we awaken to our True Nature.
So that we can shape a world
Where children play with happy hearts and bellies,
Where yin and yang dance on equal footing
And a rainbow of relationships is relished.
Where elephants roam and mountains stay whole,
Where wildflowers and three-sister gardens bloom,
Where trees are hugged and their time is honored.
Where people leave their homelands for adventures
And refugee camps are empty.

Dearest Beloved,

May it be Your will
That my heart remains relaxed
And my mind sustained by silence,
One moment at a time.

And may it be Your will
That at the end of my days
I smile at a life well lived
Knowing that I shared my love song entirely.

Amen.

Emunah Herzog—Jew-Bu in love with Venus; German/Canadian transplant to the USA going on 56 years on the planet; novelist seeking representation to get her "babies" published; hospice nurse; activist-of-sorts working on being more playful—ha-ha-wink-wink—and co-creating the new story where even the oppressors are liberated.

Home, thawing
Polish Hill neighborhood, Pittsburgh, USA, 2018
By Hannah du Plessis

Lead Them Home
By Kelly Berg

Blow your magic on the chimes
Wake the heart of mystery
Hang yourself upon the cross
Splay your soul for all to see

Forge your way through winding trails
Wind and dust pounding your face
Rain will wash away your pain
Sleeping Lady brings you grace

Hang a hammock of your truth
Between two gently bowed oak trees
Journey past the trail's end
To the sun, the moon, the seas

Through the threshold of unknowing
Show them life in the unknown
Through the tunnels of despair
Show them where their seeds are sown

Nudge them down the rabbit hole
Guide them through the looking glass
Thaw their memories and dreams
Trapped in locked futures and cold pasts

Hand them smooth pebbles of wonder
To run through their fingertips
Send them harmonies from doves
Pull sweet songs from their own lips

Stream bright rays of light and love
Through their dusty windows of grief
Pass them rainbows of tomorrows
Hold their hand, hold their belief

Dig deep into their garden
Plant compassion in their soil
Tend to flowers long forgotten
Soothe their hands with balsam oil

Pour new hope in their foundation
Shutter fears and sweep up lies
Pave their driveways with acceptance
Burn their front door of disguise

Hurricanes of broken hearts
Turn your words into a sword
A magic blade from which you sing
Carving notes out from their chords

Build a haven from your wings
A safe place for them to land
You've been out and back before
Lead them out and back again

Fly them high into the sky
A universe to call their own
Dance with them into their dying
Fly them up and lead them home

Human in Nature
By Kerryn Elrick

Emerging green into the filtered life,
Connecting with community to build
Essential foundations —
Jewel-colored wings encasing tender hopes.

Alive with possibilities,
Precision whiskers and cat-like intuition
Hone in
To the calls of an untethered heart.

At your strongest,
Sinews stretch and muscles drive you forward,
Camouflage
Bringing both freedom and boundaries.

But human in nature —
What do you know about the earth without asking?
What can you see without using your eyes?
What can you lift when your arms are dead weight?
What peaks can you reach with only instinct to guide you?

Human in nature —
What peaks can you reach?

I live with my family and an assortment of animals, amongst the trees and wildlife, not far from the beach in Victoria, Australia. All of us are at different stages in our lives. Some of us are old and achy. Some of us are young, sparky and adorably naive. And some of us are just happy for the moment beetling about in the garden. I was thinking about our different stages in life when I wrote this poem.

Way of Life—The Artist's Way
(A Villanelle)
By Elina van der Heijden

Write colors of your world with light
When on your path you go
Draw skies in blues and clouds in white

Capture views when on a height
See crane's bill in a low
Write colors of your world with light

Open hearts with every sight
Inspire and spread the glow
Draw skies in reds and clouds in white

Even in your soul's dark night
In times when you don't know
Draw colors of your world with light

Lift your eyes, see stars shine bright
Find wonders down below
Draw skies in greens and clouds in white

Show life's beauty in its might
There's so much more to grow
Write colors of your world with light
Draw skies in gold and clouds in white

Elina van der Heijden loves language, colors and images. She's a translator and a Reiki master who finds great joy in all kinds of creative expression. In her photography she lets herself be guided by her motto 'Beauty is all around.' You can find some of her work at <u>epvdh.blogspot.com.</u>

Skies in Gold
By Elina van der Heijden

In and After
By Mary Cartledgehayes

I. In the Stillness

Nothing
is
everything.

Everything
is
nothing?

II. After the Stillness

Every thing —
the sight in a dream of my mother laughing
a whiff of skunk
the burbly purr of the green-eyed cat —
is something.

Some thing —
Spirit's dance in the corona the day the moon
    overcame the sun
the taste of my love
the persistent pleasure of his taut silken skin
    beneath my hand —
is everything.

Mary Cartledgehayes is a writer, mystic, and artist.

Out of Exile
By Elsa Wolman Katana

So you know how when you dive into the lake and you become me/he and you swim down and it becomes sea and you notice there's a black snake accompanying you/me and we land in the desert and are climbing a dune and are met by the Elder/he and turn to see the Sphinx/she and walk towards her and he/you/me enter a cavernous room and you/me/he start to dance with the snake to a drum that quiets the earth and she/you/me enters through he and how now we sit on the dome of the world you/me and he holding a raven haired she surveying the exile and she/you/me says to he I will be the last to leave. And we/me/you/he and a black snake we return to she with the Elder's blessing I love you/her/me. That!

Elsa has a MFA degree in painting. But words are her first love. She writes to share the grace and challenge of this astonishing human experience. A wayfinder in the Martha Beck tradition, you can find her at www.elsakatana.com.

When I Am Free
By Kathy McKinley

Please take these stories from my mind
And place them deep within the earth
Where they may rest in sacred silence
Through all eternity.

Please take these ghosts from my past
And scatter them into space
Where they will disappear into another galaxy
And be transformed into a brilliant Star of light.

Please take the pain of this body
With all its demands and restraints
And let it soar with you in spirit
Until it is no more.

And then, when I am free…

Please let me be a wave, crashing on the shore
Please let me be the Moon, where lovers meet and kiss
Please let me be a lion, wild and on the hunt
Please let me be a scoop of earth, where children laugh and play
Please let me be a tree, with branches to the sky
Please
Let me be.

Kathy is happiest when she is walking in nature and communing with the wild and gentle creatures of the earth and ocean. She has learned a lot from them.

Self-Portrait
By Johanne Lila Larsen

I call canon in the rock cathedral
By Lara O'Connor

I call canon in the rock cathedral. I bring chapel to the moss. Angels are playing air guitar, headbanging in the brush. This is today's song:

Grandmothers, take me home. Let me curl up by the fire, cry for everything lost. Tug off my boots, shake your head over the miles. Bring mercy to the corners. Put the trees on the phone.

The longing hangs on my legs, keening faintly like a tired child.

Home.

Home.

Take the A train: a shaft of light through trees. B train: the softening of the heart before sorrow. C, naked prayer. D, desperation. E, if we catch it, everlasting joy.

Let me get there fast by car, sunroof open, radio on, heat blasting.

Let me go there slowly, walking through woods, stooping under mushrooms to share forest tea.

Let me wander in the rain, barefoot and underdressed, my wineglass filling with water, toasting myself and every other queen. Bring me nose to pink nose with wild creatures, teach me how dirt sings its unfolding to the mole.

Just, tell me you love me. That camp will be over, and I'll be home soon.

I miss you.

I need a postcard, or visitation.

Call the Holy Spirit for a taxi. Pick me up—the usual. Bathroom floor.

I've cried longing for so many years, I'm hoarse. Some days I only reach for God with one arm; I half try.

The longing. It suffuses and evaporates, like morning dew, an airborne tide.

What do I call for? The moment of crushed petals. The architecture of a pinecone. Always, the smell of the ocean, the mother sound.

Sometimes heaven is a person's chest—exactly the one you can't get back to. Yearning becomes a glittering red and tangerine rage, a banded firework spectacular.

Then midnight blue pain. The last colors in the box. The scrape of the lathe as the night of the soul carves your bones. You are made into a work of art: sheared and shaped like water over stones.

Water over stones.

Sit and listen. This is the only sound. It is contrast.

Ever since I saw you long ago, I've wondered if you were real. So I called you when I dove into the well. I asked the favors back for every sacred thing I'd ever done. I tallied up every pure offering of my heart. I asked for the lump sum, the granddaddy miracle.

To ask to be restored to fullness, even for a moment, is to know the contours of your emptied heart. When it happens again and again, you get to know the World. Through gain and loss you learn the Braille of every life-scored heart.

I ran miles between the threshold of Life and Death. Don't let them fool you. The liminal space is neither a sliver, nor a narrow chasm. It's a fucking desert marathon.

I know this seems a rambling, slightly-less-than-holy call. But I'm an old hand at this, and no longer rush my walks with God.

We are waking up, we have overslept. It's the noon of the soul. There's joy to be done.

Lara O'Connor is the mother of three boys and caregiver to her recently disabled husband. She's a passionate cook and foodie who is new to writing. She lives in Maryland at the very top of the Chesapeake Bay.

Because we're carp. And bees. And trees. Because we are becoming dragons.
Because we are becoming truth. Color me in, make me your own.

Design by Julianne May

ACKNOWLEDGEMENTS

This anthology has been a labor of love over the course of several months, involving many able (and often anonymous) hands. We would like to first thank all the writers who have bravely and vulnerably shared some of the most intimate parts of themselves on these pages. This book is yours; this book is ours. And to those among our community who did not contribute words, we hope you see yourselves reflected here as well.

We hold a very special place in our hearts for the luminous Martha Beck, whose three-part "Write into Light" course in 2017 was the beginning of it all. Martha acted not only as a teacher but also as a mentor and friend, mobilizing a deeply bonded community and calling us to awaken fully as writers and people. She and her loving team of elves, including Rowan, Betsy, Katja, Kat, and Christina, worked tirelessly to create an immersive writing-and-living experience for students around the globe. The care with which they treated our work set the tone for how we wanted to undertake this project. We would also like to thank the inimitable Elizabeth Gilbert for sharing her wisdom and generosity of spirit with us throughout the course. To everyone at Martha Beck, Inc. (MBI) who made WIL possible, we offer our deepest thanks.

To and from the Anthology Team: we could not have asked for a more giving, loving, and sensitive group of souls to shepherd this project to fruition. How lucky we are to have found one another! The endeavor was one of true collaboration, where every voice was as vital as the next. We are all grateful for the editing efforts, insights, and spirited dedication of Blossom Lievore, Fatima Viola, Hannah du Plessis, Jessica Waite, Julianne May, Kat Soong, Laura Harbin, Lauren Oujiri, Meagan Adele Lopez, Rebecca Tolin, Tricia Elliott, and Wendy Wyatt, as well as to Cristine Reynaert, Deanna De Paoli, and Mary Walker for their thoughtful questions and generous support.

Danielle Fournier, we thank you for publishing this anthology not only with beauty but also with love. Tia Ho, your organizational prowess literally kept the boat moving forward at all times. Cynthia Rome, your ability to edit from the heart both strengthened and softened every piece. Naina Saligram, your leadership and creative vision not only inspired us but raised us all to be our better selves. This book simply would not exist without you.

A tidal wave of thanks goes to an anonymous donor for helping to fund the print edition of the book.

Finally, we express our deepest gratitude to our readers for bringing life to ink on a surface. May we forever be joined in song.

The spirit that wants to heal the earth for us—not for itself, but for us—is abroad in the human race right now. It's in you and in me with the intention to show us that "you" and "me" are an illusion. There is only "all"—all for all, always. When we wake up to that, we will save the world.

- Martha Beck, "All for All, Always"